SCHEDULED CASTES QUEST FOR LAND AND SOCIAL EQUALITY

About The Author

All throughout the professional career of more than four decades, **Dr. Harshad R.Trivedi** is engaged in theory building, empirical study and research of changing socio-cultural situation in Indian society. Starting from structural - functional study of Mers of Saurashtra, he has provided Revisit Study of Mers after 30 years and worked in various fields of public health, urbanisation, public administration, scheduled castes, tribes, other backward classes and cultural aspects.

While contributing scores of papers of empirical and theoretical nature to Indian and foreign journals, Trivedi has to his credit nearly a dozen books in English and Gujarati. This book is a sequal to his publication of Scheduled Castes Women: Studies in Exploitation; and Tribal Land Systems: Land Reform Measures and Development of Tribals, both of which are related to amelioration of socio economic conditions of deprived sections of society in modern India. Recently he studied Incidence of Dowry and Atrocities against women in Gujarat under sponsorship of Department of Woman and Child Delelopoment , Government of India, New Delhi.

Dr. Trivedi has now prepared two manuscripts on Mers, one on socio-economic survey of 12 villages with an assorted profile and second on diachremic study of Folk Art and Culture of that Vibrant community. Four monographs on the Mers is a unique contribution of the author.

SCHEDULED CASTES QUEST FOR LAND AND SOCIAL EQUALITY

HARSHAD R. TRIVEDI
Director,
Institute of Cultural and Urban Anthropology,
Ahmedabad.

Foreword by

DR. YOGENDRA MAKWANA
President,
Akhil Bharat Anusuchit Jati Parishad,
New Delhi.

CONCEPT PUBLISHING COMPANY, NEW DELHI- 110059

ISBN 81-7022-593-0

First Published 1996

Published and Printed by
Ashok Kumar Mittal
Concept Publishing Company,
A/15-16, Commercial Block, Mohan Garden,
New Delhi - 110059 (India).
Phones: 5554042, 5504042

FOREWORD

Ours is a democratic polity wherein planning has been given pivotal roll for the overall development and to establish a Socialist Society as enshrined in our Constitution. Planning is the sum total of efforts made by a number of participating Governments as well as voluntary agencies to achieve the targets fixed under the plan. This gives an opportunity to every citizen in our country to contribute his mite in policy-making and proposing programmes for the development of the country. The important elements of the community directly participating in this multi-dimentional efforts for development are various categories of leaders such as Legislators, Members of Parliament, Administrators, Social Scientists and Social Workers all engaged in nation-building activities from top to the bottom strata of the Indian Society.

We being a developing society are confronted with a number of socio-economic problems of varying magnitude. Therefore, it becomes necessary to undertake ongoing studies of problems and to try to measure the size of each problem to get a clear view of the required efforts to solve them. If timely measures are not taken, the aftereffects of such problems on various segments of the society give rise to multiple problems of maladjustment. A number of studies related to agriculture, industry and issues connected with management of natural resources, including land and human resources, call for special attention.

The Central and State Governments have framed Five Year Plans Tribal sub-Plans and Special Component Plans for required programmes and enacted laws aimed at ameliorating the conditions of the poorer sections of the society and in particular that of Scheduled Castes and Tribes. Most of the plans are action oriented but whether they have fulfilled the expectations, call for an honest appraisal. During the last quarter of the century, it is difficult to affirm with confidence as to what extent we have achieved the development of the target groups. However, some change is apparent in their socio-economic conditions. But it is necessary to find out as how far the intended benefits have percolated down to the people of Scheduled Castes, Scheduled Tribes and Backward Classes. With this noble end in view, the Research Cell of Akhil Bharat

Anusuchit Jati Parishad intended to make objective observations on the socio-economic conditions of the Scheduled Castes in Gujarat to begin with.

The present study, "The Scheduled Castes' Quest for Land and Social Equality" aimed to achieve the goal of objective evaluation. The study was initiated with the help of financial assistance from the Ministry of Home Affairs, Government of India, New Delhi. We are grateful to the Government of India for the grant-in-aid to undertake the study for which Dr. H.R. Trivedi was appointed. We hope that the results and recommendations of the survey will provide a sense of direction and guidance to the concerned authorities who are engaged in the work of the development of Scheduled Castes.

It should be reiterated that there is a great need for dispassionate approach to the issues involved in creating a viable programme for the socio-economic development of depressed classes today. In formulating any policy or legislation for the down-trodden people, an objective survey of the socio-economic condition will serve as a compass to measure the change. The field data collected and processed by scientific research methods would be helpful in achieving the goal of fact-finding mission set forth by us. The conclusions derived would certainly help in devicing new strategies of planning and implementation.

It is needless to emphasise here that the research workers, who collected valuable data for us, adopted scientific approach to conduct this survey. They left aside all bias and preconceived notions so that the findings and recommendations are based on reliable empirical data. The universe of the study and survey was cerefully marked out and selection of the samples at district, taluka, village and family levels were made on scientific lines.

We can bring about salutary changes in the lifestyle of the depressed people and help them in raising their plight above age old disparity if we are really serious. The ultimate goal, however, should be to bring them above poverty line and thereby accomplish the greatest good of the greatest number. There is no other way to achieve the noble goal of socialistic pattern of the society dear to the father of the nation and to our first Prime Minister Pandit Jawaharlal Nehru and so also to Indiraji.

The aim of this research study was comprehensive and all embracing. The findings of the report presented by Dr. H.R. Trivedi, the Project Director, will have far reaching impact on the *modus operandi* adopted by the administrators responsible for making suitable programmes and policies for the development of Scheduled Castes.

The efforts made by the Government of India for ameliorating the conditions of Scheduled Castes are indeed highly encouraging, right from the time of Dhebar Commission, which dealt with the problems of both the Scheduled Castes and Scheduled Tribes, the Union Government has initiated a number of special programmes for this purpose. The outstanding land-mark in the efforts made for helping these people after Dhebar Commission report was made through the Planning Commission, Government of India in organising the Seminar on "Employment of Scheduled Castes and Scheduled Tribes," in 1964. Its report was published in 1965.

I, as the President of the Akhil Bharat Anusuchit Jati Parisad, take this opportunity to express my heartfelt thanks to the then Hon'ble Minister of Home Affairs, Shri P.C. Sethi for enabling the Parishad to undertake this study by providing necessary financial assistance. I will be failing in my duty if I miss this opportunity to thank the distinguished members of the Parishad for their cooperation and help in the discharge of these responsibilities. Last but not the least, I thank Shri Narvind Gohel for looking after the coordination of the project efficiently.

YOGENDRA MAKWANA
President, Akhil Bharat
Anusuchit Jati Parishad,
New Delhi.

PREFACE

An empirical researcher is not given to come out with reflections over the subject of his research. However, I thought it appropriate to do so here. Gandhiji was uppermost in my mind, when in 1974, I took up the study of exploitation of Scheduled Castes Women on behalf of All India Harijan Sevak Sangh, Delhi in three States. Now I am presenting this report on problems of land for cultivation and land for house-sites for Scheduled Castes in Gujarat. The removal of untouchability was intricately woven with the freedom movement of Mahatma Gandhi in which I indirectly participated short of going to jail.

We seem to have forgotten the genesis of Gandhiji's real concern for the welfare of Scheduled Castes. The very concept of *Harijan* worked as a magic spell in those days of national awakening and fervour. People took it seriously and worked for removing the barriers of untouchability between castes and sub-castes. It seems that this does not appeal to the new generation of today in the same sense because the social and political climate has changed considerably.

Dr. Baba Saheb Ambedkar and the national leaders of the stature of Jawaharlal Nehru, Sardar Patel, etc., were keen to scrutinise and rationalise the problem of untouchability. They put the untouchables on a special list of depressed people having fundamental rights of equality with all high caste people in India. They were, therefore, placed on a schedule of the Indian constitution and were called Scheduled Castes in order to achieve for them a legitimate place of equality with others in course of time.

Dr. Ambedkar, the father of the Constitution of India, was extremely sore over the treatment of untouchables in our villages over the last few centuries. He wrote boldly on the subject and I need not elaborate the same here. We had greatly illtreated the Scheduled Castes in spite of the fact that they had faithfully and deligently worked for the betterment of Hindu community of which they have been an integral part. The high caste Hindus in particular and all other Indian communities in general should feel highly obliged to the Scheduled Castes, not only for keeping the village and city environment tidy, clean and hygenic, but also for providing manual labour in agriculture and semi-skilled services in the continuition of age-old traditions. It is unfortunate that we are not sensitive enough to accept the great obligations they have laid on the shoulder of all communities irrespective of caste and creed of the Indian Society.

In terms of scientific objectivity, the untouchables are culturally and genetically inseparable from other communities in Gujarat. This is amply demonstrated from the findings of the study team led by late Dr. D.N. Majumdar, Department of Anthropology, Lucknow University, Uttar Pradesh. His two research reports, (i) "Race Elements in Cultural Gujarat", 1947; and (ii) Serological Status of Castes and Tribes of Cultural Gujarat", 1948, are significant in this context. Not only the common men in Gujarat but also many scholars are unaware of the valuable findings of the reports of this eminent Indian Anthropologist. As per his findings, for instance, Bhangis in the sample of the study are racially nearer to some of the twenty one high castes and tribes studies by his research team. It means that racially most of us in Gujarat, irrespective of distinction of castes and communities, come from the identical racial stocks of men.

Among many enlightened social reformers of the freedom era, late Baba Sahib Ambedkar believed in the application of modern methods of uplifting the status of untouchables in Hindu Society. It will be most appropriate that modernisation of the Scheduled Castes is kept high on our agenda for getting them integrated with the main stream of national life.

The political leadership and intelligentsia in India are, no doubt, aware that the attitude of thanklessness towards Scheduled Castes persists even today in our society not only among Hindus but also among many other sub-castes and communities whom they have served through ages.

Certain elements of Gandhian philosophy, methods of integrating the Scheduled Castes and other depressed communities in the main stream of national life are, no doubt, praiseworthy. There are, however, certain out-dated notions of that philosophy which have to be set aside in modern perspective. It is important to note that Shri Yogendra Makwana, the President of Akhil Bharat Anusuchit Jati Parishad, New Delhi, and other eminent leaders have become torch bearers of new programme of modernising, and thereby putting the Scheduled Castes communities on equal footing with other communities. They have visualised this programme, specially for the youths of Scheduled Castes and decided to help getting them educated in technical as well as other innovative occupations. There cannot be any better approach than this for the amelioration of the pitiable conditions of the Scheduled Castes.

I am extremely grateful to Shri Yogendrabhai and Shrimati Shantaben Makwana for nominating me as the Project Director of this research study. My thanks are due to Shri G.M. Jagdish for his help and advice.

The study was carried out in 1983 in representative 4 districts of Gujarat, spreading over 16 talukas and 48 villages from where a random sample of 1800 households was taken for data collection. I am indeed grateful to Shri Narvind Gohel and Shri B.T. Dabhi for planning and supervising field-work, making threadbare micro analysis of data and tabulation. The value of the text and presentation of tabulated data have been enhanced immensely due to the help of the consultant, Shri R.D.Gandhi, former Director, Bureau of Economics and Statistics, Government of Gujarat, Gandhinagar. I am sincerely thankful to him for advice and guidance.

HARSHAD R. TRIVEDI

CONTENTS

LIST OF TABLES

1

HISTORICAL BACKGROUND

Scheduled Castes in Time Perspective

The existence of Scheduled Castes today is the outcome of historical unfair treatment (of certain groups of service class people) by the caste Hindus. In the ancient times, the under-privileged people were known by the various names such as *Avarna, Shudra, Ashprushya,* etc. All these names in the past signified that the caste Hindus looked upon them as degraded human beings worthy of all categories of so-called lower occupations. The greatest stigma attached by Hinduism is related to ritual uncleanliness of a person. It is highly ingrained in the daily life of high caste, related to the manner of religious worship and rituals associated with birth, maternity, menstruation, death, etc. This was a unique way of isolating a particular group of people serving the so-called high caste people in the Hindu society. Nowhere in the world, we find that a person is looked down upon as unclean because he undertakes certain activities of keeping the environment clean for maintenance of hygenic standards. Then how can such people in Indian society become untouchables from their very birth and are made to live as degraded for the whole of their life?

Many scholars and thinkers have tried to explore as to how this custom of untouchability has come to be practiced by the Hindus. There is no mention of such a practice in the Hindu Dharma Shashtras where one finds some historical perspective of development of Hindu ethos. Dr. Ambedkar, one of the architects of the Constitution of India, made vigorous efforts to study Hindu scriptures and to find out whether there is any mention of the practice of untouchability either in treatise called Dharmashutra or Shruti of the Hindus. The term outcaste does not indicate in any way that the Scheduled Castes are thrown out of the Hindu fold. On the contrary, it simply signifies that they do not have the privilege to mix with in day to day social life with people of other three *Varnas* based on specialised occupational structure of the society. The *Varnashrama* system of the Hindu society was conceived mainly with the view to indicate merely the division of the people on the basis of type and quality of the occupations. It did not signify that those who perform manual categories of occupations have to be considered as degraded or untouchables. "Ambedker in his own style discussed the problem of the origin of untouchables in historical context. He referred to the concept of untouchability as prevalent in Hindu society from the time of Manu till today. According to Ambedker untouchability sprang from two different attitudes, firstly, opposition to a group of depressed people and secondly, to their habits. These were expressed in (1) contempt and hatred of 'broken man' as of Buddhists by the Brahmins; and (2) persistence of beef eating habits among the 'broken men' even though it was given up by the others".[1]

As indicated by Dr. Ambedker, "The broken men hated the Brahmins because the Brahmins were the enemies of Buddhism and the Brahmins imposed untouchability upon the broken men because they would not leave Buddhism. On this reasoning, it is possible to conclude that one of the roots of untouchability lies in the hatred and contempt which the Brahmins created against those who were Buddhists".[2] It is true that the Buddhists and the Brahmins hated each other and this is one of the reasons why the untouchables regarded the Brahmins as inauspicious and did not employ them as their priests and did not even allow them to enter into their quarters. According to the former President of All India Harijan Sevak Sangh, Delhi, Shri Viogi Hari, there are references to untouchability in the sixth century of the Christian era when Buddhism was weaker and the influence of Brahmanism had revived. This seems to be the landmark from where the extreme form of untouchability was practised by the orthodox Hindus. The curse of untouchability become so severe on the life of the outcast population that all these communities were practically forced to live on the outskirts of villages and towns. Their living quarters were located in the lower part of the village habitation site which were unhygienic and susceptible to spread of diseases.

Social Reform Movements

Adi Shankaracharya is reported to have encountered an untouchable in the street of Holi city of Kashi. He changed his attitude towards them under the influence of non-dualism practised by him. Similarly, the Saint

Ramanujacharya did not accept the distinction between the Brahmin at the top and the untouchable at the bottom of the caste hierarchy of the Hindus. In the middle ages, a number of saints such as Kabir, Gyanadev, etc. preached equality among all the castes in Hindu society. In Gujarat, Narshinh Mehta, the Vaishnavait saint, used to go to the Harijan quarters and sing songs in the praise of God. Among a number of other reformist Hindu thinkers and preachers, the names of Cheitanya Maha Prabhu, Ramakrishna, Vivekananda, Dayanand, etc., denounced the ill treatment of untouchables by the caste Hindus. Swami Vivekanand had gone as far as pronouncing that it was futile to look down upon *shudras* as backward and a time would come when they will hold the position of the rulers of India. In the recent history of Gujarat, it is important to note that the Sayaji Rao Gaekwad -III of the state of Vadodara launched a vigorous drive for the removal of untouchability in the area under his state. Dr. Ambedker was the most advanced of the untouchable leaders who received full patronage for his personal development from Sayaji Rao-III. This was a kind of secular movement that was launched by the learned and most forward looking Indian prince of Gujarat. When Gandhiji returned to India in 1915 from Africa, he established his Ashram in Ahmedabad for launching agitation against the Britishers for freedom movement. He preached to the inmates of his Ashram not to practice untouchability, and at the same time he adopted an untouchable family as the inmates of his Ashram in accordance with the suggestion of, his social reform aide, Shri Thakkar Bapa.[3] His Ashram, on the bank of Sabarmati river, was also named Harijan Ashram. He wished to convey to the people that in the eyes of god there is no distinction between man and man and that all men are the "Sons of God", literally Harijans. After passing away of Mahatma Gandhi, the name of the Harijan Ashram has been changed to Gandhi Ashram by his followers. This has been looked upon by some prominent leaders of scheduled castes to be the greatest dis-service the followers of Mahatma Gandhi have done to the cause he stood for.

Definition of Scheduled Castes

It is necessary to throw some light on the manner in which the use of term Harijan is practiced by different writers on the subject. "It appears that the term 'untouchable' in common parlance refers to those people whom Mahatma Gandhi identified as Harijans. But when we use the term scheduled castes, it is not necessary that all or most of them so referred to are untouchables or Harijans. We find that the terms 'untouchable' and 'scheduled caste' are mistakenly used to indicate the same class of people... The anomalous situation leads to a lot of difficulties in perceptual understanding of the scheduled castes, but all scheduled castes may not be Harijans or untouchables"[4] The Constitution of India has been quite candid in the identification of Scheduled Castes. The census of India 1961, Volume V, for Gujarat, gives a clear understanding that religion is the main reference element on which the existence of scheduled caste rests. It says "unlike the scheduled tribes, which may belong to any religion, scheduled castes can belong either to the Hindu or the Sikh religion. Among the scheduled castes of Gujarat, only 3 persons, one male and two females are written as professing chief religion".[5] This can be due to inadequate enumeration. We may present here a working definition of the scheduled castes which calls for acceptance by those who are deeply concerned about the problem of integration of scheduled castes in the Hindu society in particular. The proposed definition reads, "All those castes, who are listed in the schedule of the Constitution of India as scheduled castes, fall into this category. From the socio-cultural point of view, the members of all scheduled castes are Hindus by birth. In the dark ages of the history, these groups of people were treated as untouchables because of certain concepts of purity and impurity. In socio-cultural sense, the elements of untouchability may not be considered *sine-qua-non* for identifying the scheduled castes. By all means and for all practical purpose, they are mostly Hindus devoted to Hindu religion".

Politics of Harijans

In 1923, a meeting was held by the Gandhian Social Workers, who had devoted their life time and energy to uplift the position of scheduled castes, named Harijans by Mahatma Gandhi. At this historical meeting, the leaders decided to establish an association called Gujarat Antyaja Seva Mandal. Devoted social workers,namely Thakkar Bapa became the President of this association and Indulal Yagnik along with Mama Phadke were appointed as Secretaries. The main purpose of this organisation was to eradicate the custom of untouchability from the Hindu society. The important measures to be undertaken were to raise social status of Harijans by allowing theme access to the water wells, temples and Dharma-shalas (meant for providing lodging facilities to the pilgrims and travellers). It was also decided that efforts should be made to educate the children of the Harijans alongwith the children of other castes without any distinction. The activities of the Seva Mandal were vigorously taken up by the noted social reformers, and a time came when it created a very decisive impact on favourable attitude of the caste Hindus towars the Harijans. A number of conferences were held specially to propogate this reform programme of the Seva Mandal. The social workers went from village to village to find out the difficulties encountered by the Harijans. The movement of Harijan upliftment initiated by Mahatma Gandhi spread in many other provinces in India. Dr. Ambedker led the *Satyagraha* movement for entry into the temple of Guruvayur, located at Vaikam in Malabar. This was fully supported by Mahatma Gandhi and it become a great success.

When Mahatma Gandhi become victorious in his all round non-cooperation movement against the Britishers, the Round Table Conference was called in London. This was the second Round Table Conference where Dr. Ambedker was invited as the representative leader of the Harijans. Acceptance of giving special privileges and right to vote for Harijans at the time of elections was decided in the Minorities Sub-committee of the Round Table Conference. Mahatma Gandhi was firmly against the enactment of an Act by the government because he thought that it would result into disruption of the Hindu society as a whole. Gandhiji was imprisoned into the Yaravada jail at Poona and he took fast unto death in order that this Act was not enacted by the British Government. Dr. Ambedker took a conciliatory attitude with respect to the feelings of Mahatma Gandhi and did not press his demand for a special Act. One of the close disciples of Mahatma Gandhi late Pyrelal called this stand of Mahatma Gandhi as the Epic Fast. It created great awakening among the leaders of Hindu society, some of whom got together and established what they called Anti-Untouchability League which was later renamed as Harijan Sevak Sangh. The first President of the Harijan Sevak Sangh was the industrialist philanthrophist late Ghanshyamdas Birla. The Secretary of this league was late Thakkar Bapa. The term Harijan for the so-called depressed class became fully accepted in the socio-political climate of India after the establishment of this new institution.

Constitutional Protection to Scheduled Castes

According to the 8th Schedule of Indian Constitution, scheduled castes are recognised and identified as weaker sections of society. The President of India issued two constitutional orders, one for scheduled castes and another for scheduled tribes in 1950. General Introduction to the Census of India-1961, Volume V, Part-V-B-1, Gujarat. The costitutional order for recognising the scheduled castes was issued under Article 341. The important constitutional provisions and their implementation in the State of Gujarat relate to scheduled tribes also. They are, (i) prohibition of discrimination on grounds of religion, race, castes, sex or place of birth—

Article 15, (ii) equality of opportunity in matter of public employments— Article 16, (iii) abolition of untouchability — Article 17, (iv) prohibition of traffic in human beings and forced labour or bonded labour— Article 23, (v) protection of interest of minorities by religion, race, caste, language against bar on the admission to educational institutions —Article 29, (vi) protection of educational and economic interest — Article 46, (vii) equal justice and free legal aid and protection against atrocities— Article 39, (viii) reservation of seats for scheduled castes/scheduled tribes in the House of the People — Article 330; and in the Legislative Assemblies of the States — Article 332.

> "Implementation of the above Costitutional provisions has been enhanced by the appointment of Commissioner for Scheduled Castes and Scheduled Tribes and the institution of various commissions from time to time under the Article 338 and Article 340 respectively".[6]

The Government of Gujarat authorised senior officers at the district, taluka and village levels to issue certificates to the persons of scheduled caste communities so that they become eligible to avail of special privileges conferred upon them by the Constitution. The Sarpanch of a village panchayat, who is the elected representative of the people, is entitled to issue such certificates in favour of scheduled caste persons. The candidates of scheduled castes applying various kinds of services and posts in public sector industries, nationalised banks and government administration have been made eligible in order to give them equality of opportunity in matters of public employments. During the year 1976, the State Employment Exchanges recorded 26,508 Registration cases for the placement in jobs. Of these applications, 1,910 placements were effected. The Employment Exchanges were also instrumental in issuing notifications to as many as 546 reserved vacancies of which 262 were filled in. In fact, the overall slow rate of development affected the employment opportunities available to the people at large. It affected the scheduled castes also. During the reference year, 51,349 live registers were opened for scheduled caste candidates to be employed through Employment Exchanges.[7]

Situation of Untouchability in Gujarat

The problem of untouchability is still encountered in remote villages of Gujarat. Of course, it is being practised with varying degrees of differences from place to place. But this social evil continues to be there and even after more than 30 years of independence, untouchability has been observed specially with regard to use of drinking water wells and free access to scheduled castes people to tea stalls and restaurants. This problem is being tackled by the State Government by opening Harijan Cells where cases of discrimination could be lodged and necessary actions taken against guilty parties. The curse of bonded labour is also reported to be still practised by some people harbouring feudal ethos. The cases of this kind, in which the scheduled caste people are involved, is also taken care of by Harijan Cell established to give them protection from the evil of bonded labour.

As far as the educational problems of scheduled castes are concerned, they are tackled through vigorous drive of enlisting special enrollments for admission of scheduled caste children into the primary schools. In 1974-75, as many as 2,84,363 scheduled caste children were admitted in classes 1 to 4. In other words, 97 per cent of scheduled castes children in the age group of 6 to 11 were enrolled. This proportion was less by 5 per cent *i.e.* 29 per cent for the year 1973-74 for the same age groups and classes.

The percentage of enrollment of scheduled caste children for class IX and above in the age group 14 to 17 years for the year 1973-74, was 15.2 per cent but in 1974-75, it increased upto 18 per cent. It is evident that the literacy rate and its level has been going up gradually among the scheduled castes in Gujarat.[8]

A large number of scheduled caste people are living in rural areas and earning their subsistence from agriculture. Hardly a few of them have sufficient land for cultivation. Therefore, a very large section of the scheduled castes work as landless labourers. "According to Census of 1971, out of 32.97 per cent recorded as workers, 6.05 per cent and 15.36 per cent scheduled caste persons worked as cultivators and landless agricultural labourers respectively. Their proportion as workers in the industrial categories of secondary sector is higher as compared to the corresponding figure for the general population with special reference to household industries. This is because they are also found to be engaged in many other traditional occupations such as weaving, tanning and cleaning of hides, making palm-leaf mats, brooms and such other articles".[9] This means that if the scheduled castes have to be made economically self-sufficient, it is necessary that the surplus land is made available to them for occupancy right as cultivators. If we are able to provide economic landholding to the scheduled castes in rural areas, we will be able to built up the household economy of this section of the people who have been working hard to strengthen the very foundation of our agro-based economic structure.

It seems that we shall have to be very vigilant about the prevention of atrocities on Harijans, specially in the rural areas. According to the report of the Commissioner of Scheduled Castes and Scheduled Tribes for 1976-77 (p. 107), during implementation of 20 Point Programme and other progressive measures in favour of weaker sections, the people of vested interest were enraged. This led to a number of cases of harrassment and atrocities against the people belonging to scheduled castes. In 1975, there were only 184 cases, which rose to 203 in 1976. Again during 1977-78, there were 209 cases of atrocities which led to killing of 19 persons of scheduled castes.

The reservation of seats for scheduled castes in the Lok Sabha and the Legislative Assembly of the State of Gujarat have been made on the basis of Delimination Order (Amendment) Act 1976. According to the recommendation of the Election Commissioner, there have been 2 scheduled castes seats out of 24 in the Lok Sabha and 13 seats out of 168 in Legislative Assembly in Gujarat. These reservations are proportionate to the population concentration in different regions and their constituencies. In local self-governments such as Municipal Corporation, Nagar Panchayat, Jilla Parishad, Taluka and Village Panchayat, seats are reserved for scheduled caste candidates. The awareness among the members of the scheduled caste communities about their rights and privileges has increased many-fold and they are able to play a useful role in decision making process through government and semi-government institutions.

The Latest Position Regarding Land for Cultivation and House Sites

The problem of equitable distribution of land for cultivation to scheduled castes in particular is of crucial importance. This is the main focus of the present study also. It is, therefore, necessary to throw some light on the extent of benefit received by the scheduled caste people from the enactment of various kinds of land reforms and legislations. The enlightened thinkers and planners of the country thought that the introduction of tenancy legislation, land ceiling act, abolition of *Jagirdari System,* etc., would be able to create surplus land and suitable conditions for equitable distribution of land among the landless labourers in rural areas. The idea was that the tillers of the soil should get a fair deal and return from their labour. This is possible only if the cultivator becomes the bonafide landholder of the land he cultivates.

It is enlightening to learn from Yogendra Makwana, President of the Akhil Bharat Anusuchit Jati Parishad, New Delhi, regarding the position of landholding associated with the people of backward class. "In spite of the plethora of land laws clubbed together under the label of 'Land Reforms Acts', it seems we have not yet been able to solve the problem and we are nowhere near its solution. Inequalities of agricultural holdings are as much in evidence today as they were in the days of British Raj. 54.6 per cent of the agriculturists hold less than 1 hectare (*marginal farmer*); 18 per cent holds more than one hectare, but less than 2 hectres (*small farmers*), while 14.3 per cent holds 2 or 4 hectares (*semi-medium farmers*). The medium farmers, whose holdings are between 4 to 10 hectares, constitute 10.1 per cent, whereas the large or big farmers having holdings of 10 hectares and above are only 3 per cent of total agriculturists".[10]

If this is the position of the general class of the landless labourers in the country, one can understand how miserable it would be for the scheduled castes to hold land for self-cultivation and subsistence. Our purpose here is to throw valuable light on the extent to which the small and marginal farmers and specially the people of the scheduled castes have been able to get any tangible benefit from the schemes prepared for the welfare of the scheduled castes in Gujarat.

It is estimated that 66.0 per cent of the bonded labourers of the country belong to the scheduled castes and most of them are working as landless labourers. The wages fixed by the government for payment to the people below poverty line are to be denied to them. In most of the cases, however, the minimum wages are not paid to them and when they ask for justice, they are threatened with violent consequences. All kinds of atrocities committed specially against the scheduled castes in the rural areas have naturally their roots in the desire to exploit these people by economically well-to-do persons. As per the standard adopted by the Planning Commission, those whose monthly income is below Rs. 69 in rural areas and below Rs. 88 in urban areas in relation to the price index of 1979-80 can be described as those living below the poverty line. "According to the National Sample Survey findings, 50.82 per cent of the rural population and 38.19 per cent of the urban population technically fall in the category of the people below poverty line. It is not surprising that the overwhelming majority of the people below poverty line belongs to the scheduled castes and they constitute the core of the problem of poverty in India.[11]

While making a hurried survey of the rest of the population of scheduled castes in different districts of Gujarat, one finds that their growth rate had increased instead of declining over the last three decades. It was so in spite of the fact that the government is spending crores of rupees on family planning in rural areas. This is one of the reasons why it is difficult to make a dent in the economic development of the scheduled castes in Gujarat. It seems very difficult to bring them out of the viscious circle of falling into the category of low paid agricultural labourers. "According to the data collected by the State Government for the special component plan for 1981-82, 59.0 per cent of the scheduled castes population were working as agricultural labourers, 12.0 per cent were following their hereditary profession like weaving, tanning of hides and shoe making, 80 per cent were absorbed in service and barely 11.0 per cent were cultivatiors".[12] Among these cultivators, very few had enough land to support families and had, therefore, to undertake seasonal migration for maintaining their families during the non-agricultural season.

It is heartening to note that the Government of India, Planning Commission instituted a working group in order to get a clear perspective of developmental efforts to be made for scheduled castes in India. This group prepared its report for 1980-85 wherein detailed programmes of tasks and guidelines for approaches and methods of implementation of economic and educational development programmes have been worked out. This was done under Special Component Plan in the light of human resources development including planning for social services, minimum needs programme and provision of institutional finances in order to make necessary arrangements for implementing the programme. The emphasis of the Special Component Plan has been on creating necessary stimulas for the growth of secondary sectors of economy wherein the people of the scheduled castes can be absorbed.

It is necessary that the scheduled castes people, who are surplus in rural areas, are helped to get into the allied sectors of economy and unorganised industrial activities so that their purchasing power can be stepped up over a period of time. This is the best way to ensure socio-economic integration of the scheduled castes people in the wider frame-work of social relationship. The problem of untouchability shall certainly disappear quickly as soon as we are able to help the scheduled castes attain economic equality with the people who have already crossed the poverty line.

REFERENCES

1. Ambedkar, B.R., *The Untouchables*, Amrit Book Co., New Delhi, 1948, p. 78. H.R. Trivedi, *Scheduled Caste Women: Studies in Exploitation*, Concept Publishing Company, New Delhi, 1977, pp. 16-17.
2. Dr. Ambedkar, *Ibid.*
3. Dahyabhai Naik, *Gujaratman Harijan Kalyan Pravrutti*, (in Gujarati) Govt. Central

Press, Gandhinagar, 1975, p. 5.
4. Trivedi, *Op.cit.* p. 19.
5. *Census of India-1961*, Vol. V, Gujarat, Part V-B-I.
6. Trivedi, H.R. and S.K. Bhakta, "Implimentations of Social Legislation Pertaining to Scheduled Castes in Gujarat", in *Social Administration, Development and Change*, Editors: T.N. Chaturvedi, S.K. Chandra, Indian Institute of Public Administration, New Delhi, 1980, p. 117.
7. Trivedi and Bhakta, *Op. cit.* p. 118.
8. Trivedi and Bhakta, *Op. cit.* p. 120.
9. Trivedi and Bhakta, *Op. cit.* p. 121.
10. Yogendra Makwana, "How Dark is the Shadow", *Parishad Sandesh*, Vol.I, No. 5, New Delhi, 1983, p.11.
11. Yogendra Makwana, *Op. cit.* p. 10.
12. Shantaben Makwana, "From Lending Money to Grabbing Land," *Parishad Sandesh*, Vol. I, No.5, New Delhi, 1983, p.18.

2

OBJECTIVES AND METHODS OF STUDY

Purpose of Study

The long term purpose of making a study of this kind is to make an appraisal of the conditions under which the people of scheduled castes lived in differnet regions of India after more than a quarter century of Independence. Obviously, this cannot be done at one time with satisfaction because of a variety of situations obtained in different parts of the country. Every state has its distinctive problems of helping the depressed classes of the people to improve their lot. Some of the problems are very intricate and pervasive. Eventhough the rate of economic development at national level is quite impressive, it cannot be so at State level. Similarly, it cannot be said whether an advanced state has taken proper care of its depressed classes. It is necessary, therefore, to examine the achievements of national development in terms of positive impact on the down-trodden and weaker sections of society. This is the best way to see whether the overall rate of growth is reflected in the improved quality of living conditions of this segments of the society. We should try to identify the factors responsible for the short-fall and then device ways and means to secure better deal for these people from time to time. Firstly, we should ensure that the fruits of national development reach the depressed classes as expeditiously as possible. Secondly, we should carefully identify the factors which have been responsible in impeding the flow of benefits of developments to these people. It is here that the importance of an impartial socio-economic research becomes evident. Looking at the magnitude of the problem, very few fact finding surveys of this nature have so far been undertaken in different parts of the country. The crux of the problem is that the scheduled castes people are blissfully ignorant of various ameliorative measures flowing out of the five year plans and laws and regulations enacted specially for their benefit and advancement.

If some people are able to acquire this kind of information, it is likely that they may not be really aware of the intricacies involved in administrative procedures which can be useful to them under various legal provisions and development schemes of the Union and the State Governments. This naturally leads to frustration among these people and they are sometimes forced to give up attempts for the improvement of their miserable life. The local officers in government organisations are often lukewarm in their response to the urgent needs of the depressed classes. It is only the voluntary institutions, who can break this barrier between the administration and the poor people, can do something in order to redeem them from conditions of deprivity. The knowledge of their rights and privileges has to be disseminated in easily understandable languages so that they are able to take necessary benefits in spite of intricate maze of administrative red tape.

Place of Scheduled Castes in National Progress

As a result of Five Year Plans, spanning over a period of three decades, industrial output in the country increased many folds. A number of huge industrial units sprang up both in public and private sectors of the national economy. We, as a nation, have attained self-sufficiency in many fields of economic activities and have kept up the tempo of making headway in other fields also. One may naturally ask the question as to how many scheduled castes people were able to set up industrial units of their own and also whether any one of them became industrialist in real sense of the term.

Proceeding side by side with the economic development, there was considerable progress on the national health front also. The average longivity of the Indians was 41 years in 1961 but this increased to 54 years during 1971-81. On the other hand, the rate of mortality went down to 2.8 per cent per thousand from 14.8 in recent past. In the beginning of the last decade, the birth rate came down to 36 per thousand in the place of 41.7 in the earlier decade. The overall per capita national income increased by 1.5 per cent as a result of the improvement of living conditions of the people in general.

In the field of education, we have registered considerable development. The question that arises to a common man is to know whether the standard of education, longivity and other conditions of living have improved in the case of scheduled castes and other backward communities. It will be useful to know the extent to which the birth rate increased or declined in their case. The growth rate of per capita income of the scheduled castes people should be compared with the same pertaining to people of higher castes in the society. It is evident that we are at a stage of development where a searching inquiry needs to be made in order to measure the extent of benefit of industrialisation which might have percolated to different groups in different degrees in rural areas. Whether these processes have improved the lives of the depressed classes needs to be specially investigated. We may list important reasons why such a fact finding study was overdue, in the following points:

(i) The proportion of scheduled castes in the class of agricultural landless labourers is very high and the proportion of land holding cultivators among the scheduled castes is dwindling. Moreover, other traditional occupations of many scheduled castes have been destroyed on account of various reasons.

(ii) The process of exploitation of scheduled castes in rural areas by big landholders continues unabated. The policy of land to the tiller has been converted into a ridiculous farce by vested interests, possibly in connivance with government machinery.

(iii) There are frequent instances of atrocities committed on members of scheduled castes in rural areas. The powerful sections of landlords dictate their own terms to landless labourers and at the same time harass them in all possible ways including molestations and rape of women.

(iv) Increasing phenomenon of mortgaging land and other assets of scheduled castes to moneyed parties in rural areas deserves serious attention of the authorities. The money lenders get the agreements written on ordinary stamp papers against valuable documents of land holdings of members of scheduled castes who go to borrow money.

There are many issues other than the outstanding ones listed above and for which a scientific assessment and evaluation is absolutely necessary. However, it should be noted that the government of Gujarat has already launched a special programme to help the scheduled castes people living below the poverty line to improve their lot and cross the barrier of poverty line.

The various types of ameliorative schemes for the improvement of the conditins of the scheduled castes were planned earlier on behalf of the government under the programme of social development. The departments of social welfare of the government were making a special effort to implement programmes of benefit to these people. In April 1975, the then Prime Minister of India, Smt. Indira Gandhi made it clear to the State Ministers of Social Welfare that the old practice of helping the scheduled castes through the government needs to be modified. In view of this, the Planning Commission and the Ministry of Home Affairs recommended that special provisions should be made in the programme of development in different departments to allocate 7 per cent of the budget for the development of scheduled castes. In this direction, a concrete step was taken to implement this policy in the form of "Special Component Plan for Scheduled Castes". It was decided that during 5 years of the 6th plan, every State should make concerted efforts to raise 50.00 per cent of the people of scheduled castes above the poverty line. We shall go into the details of this programme in subsequent chapters.

The Special Component Plan was implemented for scheduled castes in 1980-81 by the State Government . It was estimated that out of 18.25 lacs of scheduled castes people, a minimum of 50.00 per cent of the population should be helped in such a way that they are able to come above the poverty line. The Social Welfare Department of the Government of Gujarat initiated a survey in 1411 villages, each having 250 members of scheduled castes. This amounted to about 50.00 per cent of the scheduled castes population in Gujarat. It was planned that every year 20.00 per cent of the villages from this group be selected for implementing Special Component Plan. In the year 1980-81, 285 villages were selected for this purpose by the Social Welfare Department of the Government. In 1981-82, this task of survey was assigned to Tribal Research and Training Institute of the Gujarat Vidyapith, Ahmedabad. In this survey, additional 316 villages were covered.

Objectives of Study

The Department of Scheduled Castes and Backward Classes in the Ministry of Home Affairs, was consulted before finalising the objectives of the present study. Even the design of sample selection and methods of research were discussed as much in detail as possible with the senior officers of the department. The list of objectives as approved by the government resolution sanctioning the grant for the project is presented in the following points:

The study had be conducted in the State of Gujarat, covering the following objectives—

1. To assess the extent of benefits made available to scheduled castes as a result of the execution of special legislative enactments such as Land Ceiling Act, Tenancy Act, Abolition of Jagiradari Act, and other Acts, related to matters of land revenue, grazing land and allotment of Government waste lands.
2. To ascertain the quantum (and proportion) of lands received by the scheduled castes from the ancestors and/or by various legislations and allotment of Government waste lands, and to find out how much of these lands continue to be in possession of members of scheduled castes.
3. (a) To suggest remedial measures for restoration of lands to the scheduled castes, in case they have been deprived unlawfully of any land received by them through measures referred to at point 1 above.

   (b) To suggest measures to prevent loss of land in respect of lands, other than those received through legislative measures and Government allotment.
4. To examine the legality and other aspects of the mortgage deeds made by other parties with the scheduled castes and to suggest ways and means whereby loopholes facilitating deprivation of scheduled castes of their lands can be detected and plugged.
5. To ascertain the causes of crime against scheduled castes with special reference to land problem and to suggest methods of overcoming the same.
6. To find out how far the schemes of allotting house-sites to scheduled castes were successful. What proportion of funds earmarked for this purpose had been utilised for the same, and to suggest specific steps necessary to accelerate this process in the right direction.
7. To ascertain and find out the benefits received from the Special Component Plan for scheduled castes and to suggest measures to improve its implementation.
8. To attempt in broad terms, an overall evaluation of the socio-economic conditions of scheduled castes.
9. To assess developmental needs of scheduled castes families and their basis with regard outlays required for the purpose.

We have tried to give full justice to the problems of SCs while covering the various aspects of the objectives listed above.

Methods of Study

Broadly speaking, the universe of this study is related to the whole of Gujarat. We hope that inspite of certain distinguishing features of scheduled castes to be found from the sample districts selected on rational basis, the picture that emerges from the analysis of information will be representative of the scheduled castes in the State. Apart from the manner, in which samples have been selected for investigation, a number of tools were evolved in order to give justice to the objectives determined for this study. We shall now throw light on the general design of the study including sample selection and preparation of tools and techniques of investigation in the following paras.

It may be noted that the state of Gujarat is devided into 19 districts as given in Appendix - I. Of these, the districts of Dangs, Valsad, Surat, Bharuch and Panchmahals are predominently tribal in population. The districts of Sabarkantha, Banaskantha and Baroda have several areas predominated by the population of the scheduled tribes. All these areas and certain pockets of tribals have been covered for the programme of development under Tribal Area Sub-Plan of the Government of Gujarat. This is important to note because in the above areas, the population of the scheduled castes on whom the present study is concentrated is negligible. In brief, we have 8 districts in the State of Gujarat, where it was not profitable to extend the study of the problems of the scheduled castes. In the remaining 11 districts, the population of scheduled castes is found to be of varying degrees of concentration. It is from this group that we have selected four districts on the basis of census data.

In Appendix II, we have presented the taluka-wise population of scheduled castes in all the districts of Gujarat. This is based on the census of 1981. The Appendix also gives inter-taluka and intra-taluka percentages of population. Having done this, we have worked out the distribution of meaningful range of percentages of scheduled castes population. This has been presented below in tabular form. The basic approach to this kind of classification is to see that the selection is based on three criteria, *viz*. high, medium and low groupings of scheduled castes population by percentages.

Ranges of population by percentages	*No. of districts*
0.0 to 6.0%	7
6.0 to 11.0%	11
More than 11%	1

It can be seen from the above that there are 7 districts in the low population percentage group. It was decided to select one district in order to give representation to this group in the study. The second medium group consists of 11 districts which is the largest group according to the percentage of scheduled castes population. It was thought appropriate to give representation to two districts from this group. In the 3rd group, with the highest percentage of scheduled castes population, we have only one district, *viz.*, Ahmedabad District.

In the first group, we thought it necessary to select the district of Kaira having highest scheduled castes population in relation to other districts of the group. In the second group, it was considered appropriate to select one district having lowest percentage of scheduled castes population and another with the highest percentage. These two districts are Mehsana and Surendranagar respectively. In the third group, there was no alternative choice for selection since Ahmedabad district was the only one that represented highest population of the scheduled castes.

The names of sample districts and talukas selected on the basis of high, medium and low percentages of scheduled castes population are presented in the following table:

Sr. No.	Name of District	Taluka having highest SC population	Taluka having medium SC population	Taluka having lowest SC population
1.	Ahmedabad	Dholka	Dhandhuka Viramgam	Dehgam
2.	Mehsana	Sami	Sidhpur Harij	Vijapur
3.	Kaira	Khambhat	Kapadwanj Petlad	Anand
4.	Surendranagar nagar.	Dasada	Wadhwan Muli	Halvad

It can be seen further from Appendix-II that the total number of talukas in all the 4 districts selected as samples are 37. From this it was decided to select 16 representative talukas in terms of 4 talukas from each sample districts. From each of the sample talukas, it was decided to select three villages and from each village it was decided to select five households by adopting random sample method of selection. The pattern of selection of sample talukas, villages and households is presented in tabular form below:

The total number of 48 villages thus become the focus of the intensive study undertaken by us. The unit of observation is the household which makes a total of 240 samples from the universe of 16 talukas in 4 districts.

Sample districts	No. of sample talukas	Sample villages	Sample households
Ahmedabad	4	12	60
Kaira	4	12	60
Mehsana	4	12	60
Surendranagar	4	12	60
Total	16	48	240

It is interesting to note that between 1961 to 1971 and 1981 the district of Surendranagar had shown significant rise in the percentage of scheduled castes population from 4.0 per cent to 10.87 per cent. In the district of Ahmedabad the percentage of scheduled castes population had shown exceptional decline from 16.60 per cent in 1961 to 10.93 per cent in 1971 and 11.27 per cent in 1981.* In the other two districts of Mehsana and Kaira also, the trend was towards the decline of scheduled castes population by about 2.00 per cent between 1961 to 1971 and 1981.

In Appendix-III we have presented 4 separate statements showing list of sample talukas and villages from Ahmedabad, Kaira, Mehsana and Surendranagar districts respectively. The status of villages by low, medium and high percentages of SC population to total are also indicated.

Techniques and Tools of Investigation

Most of the data collected for this study was from interviews of the heads of the households. For these, a household schedule was prepared. Part-A was meant to elicit information from the respondents on various problems of land for cultivation and related socio-economic variables. Part-B of the schedule was prepared in order to get information on the problems of house-sites as well as participation in co-operative societies, police protection, benefits of component plans and the conditions of landless labourers in the sample villages.

Before this main household schedule was canvassed for eliciting detailed information from the respondents, other complementary and supplementary proforma and schedules were used for collecting background information and making qualitative assessment of the situation. They were Village Form, Opinion Schedule and semi-structured questions on social workers.

* This appearance of decline in SC population may be due to concealment of household identity by adopting high caste surnames under the guise of social reform and conversion to Christianity.

3

A PROFILE OF SCHEDULED CASTES IN VILLAGES

Introduction

In this chapter, we shall throw light on some aspects of the position of the scheduled castes in villages selected for the purpose of this study. The field data was collected in July-August 1983. As referred to earlier, a special schedule called Village Data Form was devised with a view to get background knowledge of the sample villages in all the four districts. It seems reasonable to think that the picture, which emerges from the presentation of tabulated data, provides a kind of general picture of the position of scheduled castes in select 4 districts also.

It may be noted at the outset that the total number of sample villages comes to be 48 and the total number of households of the scheduled castes based on special census collected by the Field Investigators comes to be 1782. We shall throw light on some important aspects of socio-cultural characteristics of these sample villages and scheduled castes households in the following pages.

Before we analyse the background information on sample villages and sample households, it will be useful to get a broad picture of the size of scheduled castes population in all the 4 districts under study. This data has been derived from the Census of 1981 and it is presented in a highly condensed form in Table 3.1. The idea is to give a general picture of the scheduled castes population in terms of high, medium and low percentages of shceduled castes in different sets of villages. The consolidated view of the data indicates that out of the total of 1487 villages in all the 4 districts, there were 31 villages having more than 31.00 per cent of scheduled castes population. This comes to be 2.08 per cent of the total number of villages.

TABLE 3.1: Number of Villages with Percentage of Scheduled Castes Population

(Based on Census 1981)

Sr. No.	District	No. of villages with nil population of S.C.	Villages with 0.0% to 5.0% of S.C.	Villages with 6.0% to 10.0% of S.C.	Villages with 11.0 % to 15.0% of S.C.	Villages with 16.0% to 20.0% of S.C.	Villages with 21.0% to 30.0% of S.C.	Villages with 31.0% to 40.0% of S.C.	Villages with 41.0% to 50.0% of S.C.	Villages with more than 50.0% of S.C.	Total No.of villages.
1.	Ahmedabad	73	88	105	97	65	59	13	2	—	502
2.	Kaira	60	133	126	45	31	19	2	1	1	418
3.	Mehsana	13	58	120	73	27	14	4	—	—	309
4.	Surendranagar	46	42	51	44	36	31	4	2	2	258
	Total	192	321	402	259	159	123	23	5	3	1487

Consolidated View— Villages with high, medium and low groupings of percentages of S.C. population.

Total No. of villages	High group villages with more than 31.00%	Medium group villages with 16.00% to 30.00%	Low group villages with 0.00% to 15.00%	Villages without S.C.
1487 100.0	31 2.08	282 18.98	982 66.04	192 12.91

Secondly, there were 282 villages amounting to 18.98 per cent of the villages where the concentration of scheduled castes population was 16.00 to 30.00 per cent. In the third group with low percentages of scheduled castes in relation to others, we have had 982 villages which amounted to 66.04 per cent of the total number of villages in all the 4 districts. Lastly, it is significant to note that there were 192 villages amounting to 12.91 per cent of the total number of villages, where scheduled castes people were not to be found at all.

General Information from Village Data

Now we shall deal with the general information derived from the Village Form, and presented in Table 3.2 to 3.11. Let us start with Table 3.2. So far as the representation of various sub-castes of scheduled castes is concerned, we have out of 1782 households, 839 Vankar, 571 Chamar, 267 Valmiki, 64 Garoda, 34 Senva, 4 Turi and 3 Barot. It is interesting to note from this table that the Senva, Turi and Barot sub-castes were found mainly in the Ahmedabad and Mehsana districts. Not only this, they were very small in number as compared to the total number of scheduled castes households to be found in sample villages. Another important feature is that out of the largest number of 839 Vankar households, 40.00 per cent were to be found only in the villages of Surendranagar district. The district of Ahmedabad also had a high share of Vankar households. Among the Chamar households numbering 571, Kaira had 44.00 per cent and Ahmedabad 28.37 percent. With regard to the Valmik households, we find that out of 267, 47.57 per cent were to be found in the sample villages of Kaira district. In the district of Ahmedabad and Mehsana, they were considerably low amounting to 14.61 per cent and 16.10 per cent respectively in sample villages. It is interesting to note that among 64 households of Garoda Brahmins, 68.75 per cent were to be found in the district of Kaira and the percentage of these sub-castes in Ahmedabad and Surendranagar sample villages was considerably low.

Scheduled Castes Land-Holders in Sample Villages

Table 3.3 throws light on the position of scheduled castes land-holders in sample villages. The total number of land-holders were 433 which amounts to 24.30 per cent of the scheduled castes households numbering 1782. Of these, 16.05 per cent had heriditary land, 2.58 per cent government waste land, 1.68 per cent got land under Celling Act, 0.39 per cent under Tenancy Legislation, 0.39 per cent from other government

TABLE 3.2: Number of Households by Names of SC Sub-castes

Sr. No.	District	No. of house-holds	Chamar	Vankar	Valmiki	Garoda Brahmin	Senva	Turi	Barot
1.	Ahmedabad	434	162	212	39	7	9	3	2
		24.35	28.37	25.27	14.61	10.94	26.47	75.00	66.67
2.	Kaira	578	253	153	127	44	—	—	1
		32.44	44.31	18.24	47.57	68.75	—	—	33.33
3.	Mehsana	316	101	135	43	11	25	1	—
		17.73	17.69	11.09	16.10	17.19	73.53	25.00	—
4.	Surendranagar	454	55	339	58	2	—	—	—
		25.48	9.63	40.41	21.72	3.13	—	—	—
	Total	1782	571	839	267	64	34	4	3
		100.00	100.00	100.00	100.00	100.00	100.00	100.00	100.00

souces, 0.34 per cent under 20-Point Programme, 0.28 per cent got pasture land and the same number of landholders got land from Bhooden. Under Jagirdari Abolition Act, only 0.06 per cent households got land. It is significant, however, to note that 2.24 per cent of households were able to purchase land for cultivation form others.

Table 3.4 throws light on the distribution of households of villges by various types of occupations of the heads. Out of 1782 households, 237 were farmers, 1107 households were agricultural labourers, 180 households earned living by animal husbandry and 136 were in service, 16 engaged in various types of petty crafts, 6 engaged in business and 44 did miscellaneous jobs such as labour, etc. It is interesting to note that except in the district of Kaira and Mehsana, where the scheduled castes farmers were less in number, they were considerably high in the district of Ahmedabad and Surendranagar. Among the agricultural labourers, Kaira had the highest number of scheduled castes households engaged in that work, and Mehsana had next highest number. Households industry was being practised by considerably large number of scheduled castes households in the sample villages of Surendranagar district. Those engaged in service were considerably larger in number from the scheduled castes households in the district of Kaira and Ahmedabad.

Village Level Information on Occupations, Housing and other Facilities

In Table 3.5, we have some information on the nature of houses and condition in which the scheduled castes people were living. Out of 1782 households only 21 *Pucca* houses had cement concrete roofs on their houses, while 419 had tin sheets or tiles on their houses. Of the *Kutcha* houses, just 1328 houses had tin sheets or tiles on their roofs while 18 households were having *Kutcha* roof. It is interesting to note that the housing condition of the scheduled castes households in the district of Kaira was much better. Here, 52.38 per cent of households had pucca houses with cement concrete roofs. So far as the *Pucca* houses with tin sheets or tiles were concerned, the position of scheduled castes households in the district of Ahmedabad and Surendranagar were far better. The largest number of *Kutcha* houses were to be found also in the district of Kaira which gave a significant contrast to some of those who had pucca houses. It is interesting to note that there were 18 households of scheduled castes in sample villages without satisfactory roofs over their houses, specially in the district of Ahmedabad.

The Table 3.6 throws light on facility of electricity in sample villages. There were 35 Villages out of 48 villages where electricity facility

TABLE 3.3: Land-holders by Nature and Type of Land

Sr. No.	District	Total No. of H.H.	No. of Land-holding House-holds	Hereditary	Govt. Waste	Under Ceiling	Under Tenancy	From Revenue Deptt.	Under 20 Point	Pasture	Bhoodan	Purchase	Under Jagir Abolition.
1.	Ahmedabad	434	145	104	2	19	4	—	—	5	—	10	1
			33.44	36.36	4.35	63.33	57.14			100.00		25.00	100.00
2.	Kaira	578	51	42	2	-	2	—	—	—	—	5	—
			11.78	14.69	4.35		28.57					12.50	
3.	Mehsana	316	89	58	15	3	—	5	—	—	—	8	—
			20.55	20.28	32.61	10.00		71.43				20.00	
4.	Surendra-nagar	454	148	82	27	8	1	2	6	—	5	17	—
			34.18	28.67	63.04	26.67	14.29	28.57	100.00		100.00	42.50	
Total		1782	433	286	46	30	7	7	6	5	5	40	1
			(24.30)	(16.5)	(2.58)	(2.68)	(0.39)	(0.39)	(0.34)	(0.28)	(0.28)	(2.24)	(0.6)
			100.00	100.00	100.00	100.00	100.00	100.00	100.00	100.00	100.00	100.00	100.00

TABLE 3.4 Households by Nature of Occupations

Sr. No.	District	No. of House-holds	Agriculture	Agricul-tural labour	House-hold industry	Service	Artisan	Business	Any Other
1.	Ahmedabad	434	95	203	64	43	10	—	19
			39.75	18.34	35.56	31.62	62.50	—	43.18
2.	Kaira	578	38	464	—	56	1	4	15
			15.90	41.92	—	41.18	6.25	66.67	34.09
3.	Mehsana	316	64	226	4	17	1	—	4
			26.78	20.42	2.22	12.50	6.25	—	9.09
4.	Surendranagar	454	96	214	112	20	4	2	6
			40.17	19.33	62.22	14.71	25.00	33.33	13.64
	Total	1782	239	1107	180	136	16	6	44
			100.00	100.00	100.00	100.00	100.00	100.00	100.00

TABLE 3.5 Households by Nature and Condition of Houses

Sr. No.	District	No. of Households with houses	Pucca		Kutcha	
			Cement Concrete roof	Tin Sheets/ tiles roof	Tin Sheets tiles roof	Without tin sheets or tiles roof
1.	Ahmedabad	434 24.35	6 26.57	124 29.59	286 21.60	18 100.00
2.	Kaira	578 32.44	11 52.38	74 17.66	493 37.24	-
3.	Mehsana	316 17.73	4 14.05	101 24.11	211 15.94	-
4.	Surrendranagar	454 26.04		120 28.64	334 25.23	-
	Total	1782 100.00	21 100.00	419 100.00	1324 100.00	18 100.00

TABLE 3.6 Villages With and Without Facility of Electricity and Street Light

Sr. No.	District	No. of villages	Villages with Electricity		Villages without Electricity
			Street Light in S.C. Area	No Street Light in S.C. Area	
1.	Ahmedabad	12	5 10.42	5 10.42	2 4.17
2.	Kaira	12	5 10.42	3 6.25	4 8.33
3.	Mehsana	12	5 10.42	2 4.17	5 10.42
4.	Surendernagar	12	4 8.33	6 12.50	2 4.17
	Total	48 100.00	19 39.58	16 33.33	13 27.08

was found. So far as the facility of street light in the scheduled castes localities is concerned, only 19 villages were able to provide that facility to these people. In all, there were 13 villages where electrification had not reached at all.

In Table 3.7, we have information on the number of scheduled castes households with or without the facility of electricity. Out of 1782 households of scheduled castes, there were 484 or 27.16 per cent where

TABLE 3.7 Households With and Without Facility of Electricity

Sr. No.	District	No. of Households	Households with Electricity	Households without Electricity
1.	Ahmedabad	434	125 7.00	309 17.34
2.	Kaira	578	151 8.47	427 23.96
3.	Mehsana	326	82 0.22	234 13.13
4.	Surendranagar	454	126 7.07	328 18.41
	Total	1782 100.00	484 27.16	1298 72.84

electricity had reached. A large number of scheduled castes households amounting to 72.84 per cent were without electricity.

Position of Scheduled Castes in Village Panchayats and Co-operative Institutions

The position of scheduled castes members in statutory village panchayat, where a seat for them is reserved, gave interesting reading. See Table 3.8. Out of 448 members of village panchayats in 48 villages, there were 47

TABLE 3.8 Status of Scheduled Castes in Village Panchayats

Sr. No.	District	No. of Villages	No. of Panchayat Members	No. of Scheduled Castes members
1.	Ahmedabad	12	116 25.89 (100.00)	12 25.53 (10.34)
2.	Kaira	12	125 27.90 (100.00)	9 19.15 (7.20)
3.	Mehsana	12	111 24.78 (100.00)	17 36.17 (15.32)
4.	Surendranagar	12	96 21.43 (100.00)	9 19.15 (9.38)
	Total	48	448 100.00 (100.00)	47 100.00 (10.49)

members elected from scheduled castes. Of these, the largest number were to be found in the district of Mehsana. The next largest number of scheduled castes members in panchayat in sample households was to be found in the district of Ahmedabad.

The information on membership to various kinds of co-operative societies in the sample villages throw interesting light on the awareness of the scheduled castes members for becoming members of these innovative organisations. See Table 3.9. Out of the total of 7774 members of co-operative societies of various types in 48 villages, the number of scheduled castes members to be found were only 448. Further, it is significant to note that only 130 members of the scheduled castes were able to become racipient of loans from the co-operative societies. In terms of percentage of membership of scheduled castes people in cooperative societies, they were lowest as compared to others, that is 6.48 per cent .

TABLE 3.9 Status of Scheduled Castes in Co-operative Society

Sr. No.	District	No. of Villages	No. of members in Co-operative Societies	No. of Scheduled Castes Members	Scheduled Castes Receipients of Loans
1.	Ahmedabad	12	2690 34.60 (100.00)	93 18.67 (3.46)	28 21.54 (30.11)
2.	Kaira	12	1868 24.03 (100.00)	81 16.27 (4.34)	—
3.	Mehsana	12	1381 17.76 (100.00)	40 8.03 (2.90)	15 11.45 (37.50)
4.	Surendranagar	12	1835 23.60 (100.00)	284 57.63 (15.48)	87 66.92 (30.63)
	Total	48	7774 100.00 (100.00)	448 100.00 (6.41)	130 100.00 (26.10)

Table 3.10 throws light on the position of primary school teachers and students of scheduled castes in sample villages. It is interesting to note that out of 388 teachers in the primary schools of sample villages, 59 came from scheduled castes. In the same way, out of 15493 students in the primary schools, only 1703 students came from the scheduled castes. Both in the case of scheduled castes teachers and students in primary schools,

the districts of Ahmedabad and Mehsana appear to show that the people of this community had shown progressive trend towards education. The position of scheduled castes in secondary schools is not as much encouraging as it was found to be in the case of primary schools. Table 3.11 shows that out of 45 teachers in the secondary schools of the sample villages, there were only 3 teachers from the scheduled castes to be found in the districts of Kaira and Mehsana. In the case of students there were 83 scheduled castes students out of 1765 taking secondary school education in sample villages. The district of Kaira appeared to be fairly advanced in the sense that 53.01 per cent of the scheduled castes students out of the total of 83 were taking secondary education there.

TABLE 3.10 Teachers and Students of Scheduled Castes in Primary Schools

Sr. No.	District	No. of Teachers	No.of Scheduled Castes teachers	Total No. of students	No. of Scheduled Castes students.
1.	Ahmedabad	83 21.39	23 38.98	3940 25.43	275 16.15
2.	Kaira	146 37.63	11 18.64	4850 31.30	384 22.55
3.	Mehsana	80 20.62	18 30.51	3273 21.13	387 22.72
4.	Surendranagar	79 20.36	7 11.86	3430 22.14	657 38.58
	Total	388 100.00	59 100.00	15493 100.00	1703 100.00

TABLE 3.11 Teachers and students of Scheduled Castes in Secondary Schools

Sr. No.	District	No. of Teachers	No. of Scheduled Castes teachers	No. of students	No. of Scheduled Castes students
1.	Ahmedabad	9 20.00	—	190 10.76	20 24.10
2.	Kaira	20 44.44	1 33.33	1200 67.99	44 53.01
3.	Mehsana	16 35.56	2 66.67	375 21.25	19 22.89
4.	Surrendranagar	—	—	—	
	Total:-	45 100.00	3 100.00	1765 100.00	83 100.00

4

SOCIAL ASPECTS OF SCHEDULED CASTES HOUSEHOLDS

Introduction

The total number of sub-castes of scheduled castes in Gujarat is 42. In the 4 sample districts, where the present study was conducted, we have had the representatives from Vanker, Chamar, Valmiki, Garoda, Senva and other minor sub-castes of scheduled castes. As per the study of Tribal Research and Training Centre of the Gujarat Vidyapith, Ahmedabad, conducted on behalf of the Social Welfare Department of Gujarat Government, these five sub-groups form about 80 per cent of the total scheduled castes in the state of Gujarat.

Sub-castes of Scheduled Castes

We shall here throw some additional light on the characteristics of sample population in terms of sub-castes of these people. Table 4.1 gives the distribution of households by sub-castes. Out of total of 240 households, 48.75 per cent were Vankar, 29.58 per cent Chamar, 13.75 per cent Valmiki, 3.75 per cent Garoda, 3.33 per cent Senva and the rest were Barot, Turi and others who formed only 0.83 per cent of the total sample households. We have indicated earlier that the first 4 categories of sub-castes are dominating in terms of size of population not only in sample villages, but also in the whole of Gujarat.

Table 4.2 gives detailed break-up of different sub-castes covered by the sample in terms of sex groups. Out of 1478 sample population, we had

* Term Bangi has been replaced by Valmiki, widespread and use.

TABLE 4.1 Sub-castes of Scheduled Castes in Districts

District	No. of Sample House-holds	Sub-castes of S.C. population					
		Vankar	Chamar	Valmiki	Garoda	Senva	Barot/Turi & Others
Ahmedabad	69	33	17	2	3	3	2
Kaira	60	20	21	14	5	—	—
Mehsana	60	24	25	6	—	5	—
Surendranagar	60	40	8	11	1	—	—
Total	240 100.00	117 48.75	71 29.58	33 13.75	9 3.75	8 3.33	2 0.83

50.41 per cent Vankar, having 416 males and 329 females. In the case of Chamar, we had 30.58 per cent of total population made up of 237 males and 215 females. In the group of Valmiki sub-caste, there were 11.57 per cent of members having 88 males and 83 females. The proportion of males to females in the case of Garoda was 24 to 28 and in the case of Senva it was 26 to 22.

Table 4.3 throws light on average size of population in the households of the sub-castes. The average size of Vankar and Chamar households was 6.73. The average size of Senva households was 6.00. The average size of Garoda households was nearly the same. It is significant to note that the average size of Valmiki, Barot and others was a little over 5.0. The overall average size of the sample households turned out to be 6.16.

Members of Sample House-holds

The basics on average size of the scheduled castes sample households is presented in Table 4.4. The total population of male and female in 240 households is 1478, as selected from each of the 4 districts, *viz*. Ahmedabad, Kaira, Mehsana and Surendranagar. The average size of households in all the four districts came to be 6.16 persons. But in the district of Kaira it was 5.10 persons which was the lowest; and in the district of Mehsana it was 7.10 persons, the highest in all the 4 districts.

In Table 4.5 is presented a break-up of the total population in both sexes of the scheduled castes in sample villages. We have here the size of females per thousand males which works out to be 852 for all the 4 sample districts. It may be interesting to highlight that the proportion of females for 100 males in the district of Kaira was the highest and next in the descending order came Mehsana, Ahmedabad and Surendranagar.

TABLE 4.2 Population of Households of SC Sub-castes by Sex

District	Vankar			Chamar			Valmiki			Garoda			Senva			Barot-Turi & others			Grand total		
	M	F	Total	M	F	Total	M	F	Total	M	F	Total	M	F	Total	M	F	Total	M	F	Total
Ahmedabad	126	96	222	56	50	106	8	6	14	6	11	17	12	5	17	7	3	10	215	171	386
Kaira	52	48	100	54	52	106	36	35	71	24	15	29	—	—	—	—	—	—	156	150	306
Mehsana	101	88	189	95	83	178	13	15	28	—	—	—	14	17	31	—	—	—	223	203	226
Suremdranagar	137	97	234	32	30	62	31	27	58	4	2	6	—	—	—	—	—	—	204	156	360
Total	416	329	745	237	215	452	88	83	171	24	28	52	26	22	48	7	3	10	798	680	1478
			50.41			30.58			11.57			3.52			3.25			0.68			100.00

TABLE 4.3 Population of Households of SC Sub-castes

Main Sub-Caste	No. of Sample Households	Male	Female	Total population	Average size of households
Vankar	117	416	329	745	6.37
Chamar	71	237	215	452	6.37
Valmiki	33	88	83	171	5.18
Garoda	9	24	28	52	5.78
Senva	8	26	22	48	6.00
Barot/Turi and others	2	7	3	10	5.00
Total	240	798	680	1478	6.16

TABLE 4.4 Population of Sample Households in Districts

District	No. of Sample Households	Total Population	Average size of households
Ahmedabad	60	386	6.43
Kaira	60	306	5.10
Mehsana	60	426	7.10
Surendranagar	60	360	6.00
Total	240	1478	6.16

The variation in the size of male and female population in the sample districts is likely to be related to migration of scheduled castes. Since a large number of scheduled castes were landless labourers, it was probable that these people tend to migrate to other places because of poor working relationship with the landlords whose treatment towards the landless labourers was not satisfactory.

TABLE 4.5 Population by Sex and Average Size of Households

District	No. of Households	Male	Female	Total Population	Average Size of Households	No. of Females per 1000 males
Ahmedabad	60	215	171	386	6.43	795
Kaira	60	156	150	306	5.10	962
Mehsana	60	223	203	426	7.10	910
Surendranagar	60	204	156	360	6.00	765
Total	240	798	680	1478	6.16	852

In Table 4.6, we have data showing preponderance or otherwise of males over females in sample households. It can be seen that there were 61 households of scheduled castes where number of males was higher than that of females. On the other hand, there were 115 households where the number of women was greater than the number of males. There were 64 households where the number of males and females in all the 4 sample districts was equal. From Table 4.7 we find that average size of households with excess of males over females was 6.44 members, and where there was excess of females over males, the average size of household was 6.40. On the other hand, where the proportion of males to females was equal, the average size of households came to be 5.40. This amounted to smaller the family, lesser is the difference in number of members of either sex.

The classification of sample population in terms of age group and sex has been presented in Tables 4.8 and 4.9. The Table 4.8 shows that out of 1478 population, 798 or 53.99 per cent were males, and 680 or 46.01 per cent were females. Table 4.9 gives the idea of the total number of persons distributed in terms of different age groups. The proportion of the sample population in the age group 0 to 5 years was 14.21 per cent. In the next age group of 6 to 14 years, the percentage came to be 21.85 per cent. The next age group in the total sample population of scheduled castes seems to be very significant. Here, we have had 13.72 per cent of the population falling in the age group of 15 to 23 years. After this age group, there is a sharp decline in the percentage of sample population covered by 30 to 44 years age group *i.e.* 15.90 per cent only. There is slightly less difference in the size of population in the next age group of 45 to 59 years old persons. Again after this age group, there is a sharp decline in the size of persons falling in the age group of 60 to 74 years *i.e.* 5.07 per cent only. The number of scheduled castes persons living above 74 years of age was negligible and all of them were males. The general belief that longivity among females is higher than males among human beings was found to be reversed in the case of sample population of scheduled castes under study. In any case, the general trend of longivity among scheduled castes after the age of 60 years was quite low.

In Table 4.10, we have tried to find out the size of membership in sample households. Even if some households of scheduled castes may have larger number of children, it seems reasonable to believe that where there were more than 8 members in a household, it was a joint family. Out of total of 240 households, 70 had 0 to 4 members, 113 had 5 to 7 members, 44 had 8 to 10 members and 13 had more than 11 members in the household. This shows that the largest number of 113 sample households had 5 to 7 members. They formed 47.08 per cent of the total households

TABLE 4.6 District-wise Preponderance of Males Over Females

District	Households with more females than males				Households with more males than females				Households with equal member of males to females.				Total male female size			
	No.of H. H.	M	F	Total	No. of H. H.	M	F	Total	No. of H. H.	M	F	Total	No. of H. H.	M	F	Total
Ahmedabad	14	35	56	91	30	131	66	197	16	49	49	98	60	215	171	386
Kaira	16	33	57	90	23	71	41	112	21	52	52	104	60	156	150	306
Mehsana	17	44	84	128	28	140	80	220	15	39	39	78	60	223	203	426
Surendranagar	14	32	50	82	34	141	75	216	12	31	31	62	60	204	156	360
Total	61	144	247	391 (26.45)	115	483	262	745 (50.41)	64	171	171	342 (23.14)	240	798	680	1478 (100.00)

TABLE 4.7 Sample Households by Preponderance or Otherwise of either Sex

Categories of Households by Preponderance or otherwise of either sex	No. of Sample Households	No. of Males	No. of Females	M to F Ratio	Total Population	Average size of Households.
Excess of females over males	61	144	247	1.72	391	6.40
Excess of males over females	115	483	262	0.54	741	6.44
Equal number of males and females	64	171	171	1.00	346	5.40
Total	240 (100.00)	798	680	0.85	1478	6.16

in the sample. The next largest group was of 70 households with family members ranging from 0 to 4. The type of households, which may be put in the category of joint family, were in all 44 where the number of members are 8 to 10. The households with more than 11 members were only 13. This shows albit hypothetically that there was a tendency of having more nuclear families than joint families among scheduled castes.

Marital Status and Education of Members

Table 4.11 throws light on the marital status of the members of sample households. This is given in terms of different age groups. The total number of unmarried persons was 47.29 per cent, of which 407 were males and 292 females. It is interesting to note that more than 50 per cent of the unmarried people in the age group of 15 to 29 were females. Those who were not married amounted to 728 *i.e.* 49.26 per cent of the total population in the sample. In the age group of 15 to 29 years, we have had 154 females married as against 129 males. This shows the tendency of early marriages among females of scheduled castes. It may be further noted that 3.25 per cent of members of both the sexes were found to be widowed. The phenomenon of widowhood among the scheduled castes increased in the higher age groups, and this seems to be quite acceptable. The persons who had taken divorce were only 0.20 per cent of the total sample. This appears to be rather surprising because according to the general belief, the cases of divorce are more common among scheduled castes than among other castes. But this may be due to non-reporting of remarriages that are common among them.

TABLE 4.8 District-wise Population by Age-group and Sex

District	Classification by sex and age-group																	
	0—5		6—14		15—29		30—44		45—59		60—74		74 & above		Total		Grand Total
	M	F	M	F	M	F	M	F	M	F	M	F	M	F	M	F	
Ahmedabad	26	23	49	38	72	50	26	21	27	27	14	12	1	—	215	171	386
															55.70	44.30	100.00
Kaira	13	12	26	35	52	46	31	26	20	23	12	8	2	—	156	150	306
															50.98	49.02	100.00
Mehsana	43	31	47	42	69	71	34	32	25	20	5	7	—	—	223	203	426
															54.69	47.65	100.00
Surendranagar	34	28	56	30	51	43	36	29	16	19	10	7	1	—	204	156	360
															56.67	43.82	100.00
Total	116	94	178	145	244	210	127	108	88	89	41	34	4	—	798	680	1478
															53.99	46.01	100.00

TABLE 4.9 Size of Population by Age-group and Sex

Age Groups	Male	Female	Total	Percentage
0 — 5	116	94	210	14.21
6 — 14	178	145	323	21.85
15 — 29	244	210	454	30.72
30 — 44	127	108	235	15.90
45 — 59	88	89	177	11.98
60 — 74	41	34	75	5.07
74 above	4	—	4	0.27
Total	798	680	1478	
	53.99	46.01	100.00	

TABLE 4.10 Number of Households by Strength of Members

District	No. Sample Households	Classification of Households by members				
		0 — 4	5 — 7	8 — 10	11 — 13	13 & above
Ahmedabad	60	14	28	16	1	1
Kaira	60	28	28	3	1	—
Mehsana	60	15	24	13	4	4
Surendranagar	60	13	33	12	2	—
Total	240	70	113	44	8	5
	100.00	29.17	47.08	18.33	5.42	

In Table 4.12, we have data on education among the members of sample households. It is significant to note that 44.99 per cent of persons were illiterate. In the case of the children visiting primary schools, the number appeared to be quite encouraging, in relation to the number of illiterates. The total number of primary school going children was 605, making 40.93 per cent of the total. Those who had taken education upto secondary and middle schools numbered 79 (5.35) and 52 (3.52) respectively. It shows that there was sharp drop out after primary school education. Further more, the students who studied upto graduate, post-graduate (1) and vocational diploma (1) were in all 28 which amounted to 1.90 per cent only.

TABLE 4.11 Marital Status of Household Members by Age-group

Age Group	Unmarried			Married			Widowed			Divorced			Total		
	Male	Female	Total	Male	Female	Total	Male	Female	Total	Male	Female	Total	Male	Female	Total
0 - 14	293	239	532	1		1	—	—	—	—	—	—	294	239	533 36.06
15 - 29	112	53	165	129	154	283	1	2	3	2	1	3	244	210	454 30.72
30 - 44	1	—	1	124	106	230	2	2	4	—	—	—	127	108	235 15.90
45 - 59	1	—	1	84	74	158	3	15	18	—	—	—	88	89	117 11.98
More than 60	—	—	—	36	20	56	9	14	23	—	—	—	45	34	79 5.35
Total	407	292	699 47.29	374	354	728 49.26	15	33	48 3.25	2	1	3 0.20	798 53.99	680 46.01	1478 100.00

TABLE 4.12 Education of the Members of Households by Age-group

Age-Group	Illetrate			Kinder garton			Primary			Middle			Secondary			Higher Secondary			Graduate, Post-Graduate and Vocational Diploma			Total		
	M	F	Total	M	F	Total	M	F	Total	M	F	Total	M	F	Total	M	F	Total	M	F	Total	M	F	Total
0 — 5	95	85	180	21	9	30	—	—	—	—	—	—	—	—	—	—	—	—	—	—	—	116	94	210 14.21
6 — 14	5	8	13	5	2	7	156	126	282	12	8	20	—	—	—	—	—	—	—	—	—	178	145	323 21.85
15 — 29	24	84	108	—	—	—	111	105	216	47	8	55	33	9	42	8	2	10	20	2	22	244	510	454 30.72
30 — 44	60	87	147	—	—	—	54	18	72	2	1	3	6	2	8	—	—	—	3	—	3	127	108	235 15.40
More than 45	102	115	217	—	5	5	27	3	30	1	—	1	1	—	1	—	—	—	1	—	1	133	123	256 17.32
Total	286	379	665 44.99	26	16	42 2.50	348	252	600 40.93	62	17	79 5.35	40	11	52 3.52	8	2	10 0.68	24	2	26 1.90	798 53.99	980 46.01	1478 100.00

**There were no doctor and engineers.*

5

LAND FOR CULTIVATION

Introduction

It is evident from the title of this research project that the study lays emphasis mainly on the problems of land for cultivation for the scheduled castes in Gujarat. There are many dimensions related to cultivation of land such as ownership of land, nature and quality of land, irrigation, mechanised farming, inputs necessary for good crops, cropping pattern, etc. The problem of land for cultivation is also related to another very important problem of mortgaging land by landholders indebted to the money-lenders. We shall throw light on different aspects of land mortgage in a subsequent chapter. In this chapter we shall deal in as much details as possible with the inhibiting features of the ownership and possession of land by the scheduled castes land-holders.

The sources from which the members of scheduled castes were able to acquire land need to be clearly understood. The land reform measures, implemented by the State Government after independence, have been of considerable importance in this matter. We shall also study the problems of real utility of land to scheduled castes towards the betterment of their status. The land received now from various sources such as government waste land, Bhoodan, etc., may or may not have been of any real gain to the landless labourers. It will be interesting, therefore, to throw special light on the impediments inherent in the distribution of surplus land to the members of scheduled castes in particular and landless labourers in general.

As it has been explained earlier, in the methodology adopted for the purpose of this research study, we have chosen to eliminate quite a number of districts out of total of 19 districts in the State of Gujarat because of concentration of "scheduled tribes" and others in some of those districts. In the remaining set of districts, we adopted the technique of choosing atleast one district each from those with higher and lower percentages of scheduled castes population. From other group of districts which fall in middle range according to the percentages of scheduled castes population to others, we selected two districts. It may be noted that the application of some of our findings are not applicable to the people of scheduled castes in the districts predominated relatively by tribal population.

Although it seems that the percentage of landholders among the scheduled castes as per Table 5.1 is quite impressive, its significance in terms of material gains to them is not at all meaningful. As we shall see in the subsequent sections in this chapter, there were very few scheduled castes landholders who were really unable to put land to real advantage because of various impediments. One of the problems was that of concealed mortgaging of land to the money landers of other castes. The poor landholders among the scheduled castes were sometimes deceived by the money-lenders to such an extent that their land was finally lost to the money-lender. The analysis of this phenomenon has legal implications and we shall discuss the matter at a later stage in this report. It is important to mention further that at the time of sample selection of households in villages, it was considered appropriate to make the choice of atleast one household whose land was reported to have been mortgaged.

TABLE 5.1 Households With and Without Agricultural Land

District	No. of Sample Households	Households with land on Revenue Records	Households without land
.Ahmedabad	60 100.00	30 50.00	30 50.00
Kaira	60 100.00	18 30.00	42 70.00
Mehsana	60 100.00	25 41.67	35 58.33
Surendranagar	60 100.00	32 53.33	28 46.67
Total	240 100.00	105 43.75	135 56.25

Landholders and Distribution of Land

It may be reiterated that in all the 4 sample districts, we had chosen 60 households making a total of 240. This is the universe of study and the focus of our analysis in this chapter. It is revealed from Table 5.1 that out of 240 households of the sample, 105 households had land recorded in the revenue records of the villages concerned. This bonafide landholders among the scheduled castes form 43.75 per cent of sample households. The remaining 135 households who make 56.25 per cent of the total households of the sample were landless. Their problem of livlihood and earnings from other occupations will be dicussed at a later stage. It will be appropriate to throw some light here on the landholders among different sub-castes of scheduled castes form the sample. Table 5.2 presents data on this subject. The Vankar were the highest landholders making 58.10 per cent of total of 105 landholders. The Chamar landholders were 26.67 per cent, Valmiki 11.43 per cent and Senva 3.81 per cent. The sub-castes of Garoda, Barot Turi and others were landless. It may also be interesting to note that the percentage of households of Vankar in the sample was 48.75 per cent, Chamar 29.58 per cent, Valmiki 13.75 per cent, Senva 3.33 per cent, Garoda 3.75 per cent and Barot/Turi and others made a small percentage of 0.83 only.

TABLE 5.2 Landholder and Landless Households e.g. by SC Sub-castes

Main Sub-caste	Landholder HH	Landless HH	Total number of households
Vankar	61 58.10	56 41.48	117 48.75
Chamar	28 26.67	43 31.85	71 29.58
Valmiki	12 11.43	21 15.56	33 13.75
Garoda	— 0.00	9 6.67	9 3.75
Senva	4 3.81	4 2.96	8 3.33
Barot/Turi & Others	— 0.00	2 1.48	2 0.83
Total	105 100.00	135 100.00	240 100.00

We shall now discuss various aspects of the scheduled castes households who were able to acquire land for cultivation. The Table 5.3 throws light on the average size of land holding and the total area of land held by sample households in the four districts under study. In the district of Ahemadabad, there were 30 landholders and the total area of landholding came to be 65.56 hectares, and the average landholding per household turned out to be 2.02 hectares. In the district of Kaira, 18 households had the total area of 18.55 hectares, and the average land holding was 1.06 hectares. It may be noted here that even though the average landholding in the district of Kaira was considerably low, the condition of the landholders there was likely to be good because of better fertility of land held by them. In the district of Mehsana, there were 25 landholders and the total area of landholdings came to be 49.86 hectares. The average land per household in the district of Mehsana was 2.0 hectares. That was comparable to the average landholding in Ahmedabad. The most striking of all the 4 sample districts was Surendranagar where 32 sample households were owners of land. The total area of land held by them came to be 146.28 hectares and the average size of landholding per household was 4.57 hectares. The overall average landholding of a household from the sample was 2.67 hectares. This shows that Kaira had the lowest and Surendranagar the highest size of landholding per SC household.

TABLE 5.3 Landholder With Area of Land per Household Land

District	Total No. of landholder HH	Total area of land (Hects.)	Average land-holding per household (Hects.)
Ahmedabad	30	65.56	2.02
Kaira	18	18.55	1.06
Mehsana	25	49.86	2.00
Surendranagar	32	146.28	4.57
Total	105	280.25	2.67

In Table 5.4, we have distribution of agricultural land held by the households of different SC sub-castes. It can be seen from this table that the Vankars had the largest number of 6 households owning agricultural land in the district of Surendranagar and Ahmedabad. There were 22 and 19 households owning 49.93 and 100.50 hectares of land respectively. It is significant to note that the comparative status of landholders coming from Chamar and Valmiki sub-castes was better in Surendranagar, Kaira and Ahmedabad districts. Among the Senva sub-castes, the landholders were to be found only in Mehsana and Ahmedabad districts. As indicated earlier, the other sub-castes were landless.

It will be further interesting to find out from Table 5.5, the sources from which different sub-castes of scheduled castes in the sample were

TABLE 5.4 Extent of Agricultural Land Held by SC Sub-castes

District	Total No. of Landholders	Total Area	Vankar		Chamar		Valmiki		Garoda		Senva		Barot-Turi & others	
			No. of HH	Land (Hect.)	No. of HH	Land (Hect.)	No. of HH	Land (Hect.)	No. of HH	Land (Hect.)	No. of HH	Land (Hect.)	No. of HH	Land (Hect.)
Ahmedabad	30	65.56	19	49.93	9	12.83	1	3.20	—	—	1	1.60	—	—
Kaira	18	18.55	9	12.09	3	1.61	6	4.85	—	—	—	—	—	—
Mehsana	25	49.86	11	18.92	10	26.95	1	0.69	—	—	3	3.30	—	—
Surendranagar	32	146.28	22	100.50	6	28.99	4	16.79	—	—	—	—	—	—
Total	105	280.25	61	179.44	28	70.38	12	25.53	—	—	4	4.90	—	—

TABLE 5.5 Acquision of Agricultural Land From Different Sources

Source of Land	Vankar		Chamar		Valmiki		Garoda		Senva		Barot/Turi		Total	
	No. of H.H.	Land (Hect.)	No. of H.H.	Land (Hect.)	No. of H. H.	Land (Hect.)	No. of H.H.	Land (Hect.)	No. of H.H.	Land (Hect.)	No. of H.H.	Land (Hect.)	No. of H.H.	Land (Hect.)
Hereditary	48	139.38	20	51.99	10	13.11	—	—	1	0.50	—	—	79	204.98
Under-Ceiling Act.	2	6.40	2	4.60	1	9.20	—	—	2	2.80	—	—	7	23.00
Govt. Waste Land	3	8.52	1	2.00	—	—	—	—	1	1.60	—	—	5	12.12
Under Govt. Schemes	4	12.06	—	—	—	—	—	—	—	—	—	—	4	12.06
Under Jagiradari Abolition	—	—	1	1.20	—	—	—	—	—	—	—	—	1	1.20
Under Bhoodan	1	3.45	3	8.99	1	3.22	—	—	—	—	—	—	5	15.66
Any other	3	9.63	1	1.60	—	—	—	—	—	—	—	—	4	11.23
Total	61	179.44	28	70.38	12	25.53	—	—	4	4.90	—	—	105	280.25

able to acquire land for cultivation. There were 48 households of Vankar owning hereditary land, which amounted to a total of 139.38 hectares. Some of these households also received land under Land Ceiling Act, Government schemes, Bhoodan and from waste land. Not only this, 3 Vankar households were able to become landholders mostly by purchasing 9.63 hectares from others. This indicates that the status of Vankar sub-castes with regard to land holdings was fairly respectable in all the four districts. The group of Chamar had 20 sample households having 51.99 hectares ancestral land. Some of them received land under Land Ceiling Act and also under Bhoodan movement. There was only one outstanding case of landholder among the Chamar who had possibly purchased land from others in the village. However, the landholding in this case was 1.60 hectares only. The Valmiki group had 10 households owning 13.11 hectares of land through inheritance. It is interesting to note that one household from his group was able to get 9.20 hectares of land under Land Ceiling Act. This is an outstanding record and same was the case with another household getting 3.22 hectares of land under Bhoodan. The land held by Senva group was largely received under Land Ceiling Act or from the government waste land in the villages. There was only one household with 0.50 hectares of land got through inheritance. This was not a very encouraging picture of 105 land owning households with not more than 280.25 hectares of land received from various sources.

It will be appropriate to conclude this section indicating the distribution of land among the marginal, small, medium and big farmers in all the 4 districts under study. Table 5.6 presents the data on this subject. The overall picture shows that there were 31 marginal farmers owning 17.63, 38 small farmers owning 63.43, 29 medium farmers owning 129.74 and 7 big farmers owning 96.45 hectares of land. This clearly shows that relatively smaller number of medium farmers were the owners of considerably big amount of total landholding.

Recipients of Hereditary and Non-Hereditary Land

The two broad categories of land holdings *viz.* hereditary and non-hereditary land holdings were the most significant divisions on the basis of which it will be possible to understand whether land reforms initiated after Independence of India to benefit the landless labourers in the countryside have been fruitful. With these general remarks, we may present the analysis of the data on the problems of land for scheduled castes.

Table 5.7 indicates that there were 79 households owning hereditary

TABLE 5.6 Households by Category and Size of Landholdings

District	Category of landholders								Total	
	Marginal farmer		Small farmer		Medium farmer		Big farmer			
	No. of H.H.	Area in (Hect.)	No. of H.H.	Area in (Hect.)	No. of H.H.	Area in (Hect.)	No. of H.H.	Area in (Hect.)	No. of H.H.	Area in (Hect.)
Ahmedabad	9	6.51	13	20.73	7	30.32	1	8.00	30	65.56
Kaira	11	3.90	5	8.89	2	5.76	—	—	18	18.55
Mehsana	7	3.70	14	23.49	4	22.67	—	—	25	49.86
Surendranagar	4	3.52	6	10.32	16	70.99	6	61.45	30	146.28
Total	31	17.63	38	63.43	29	129.74	7	69.45	105	280.25

Standard Categories of Landholders:
Marginal — less than 1 Hect.
Small — 1.01 to 2.51 Hect.
Medium — 2.51 to 7.50 Hect.
Big — More than 7.51 Hect.

TABLE 5.7 Households Owning Land from Hereditary and Other Sources

District	No. of H.H.	Total land (Hect.)	No. of H.H.	Hereditary land (Hect.)	No. of H.H.	Land from other sources (Hect.)
Ahmedabad	30	65.56	20	38.92	10	26.64
Kaira	18	18.55	18	18.55	—	—
Mehsana	25	49.86	21	44.71	4	5.15
Surendranagar	32	146.28	20	102.80	12	43.48
Total	105	280.25	79	204.98	26	75.27

land of the size of 204.98 hectares. Those who received land under various sources including land reform measures were 26 households. So far as the income from hereditary as well as non-hereditary land to a household was concerned, we shall present the facts and figures at a later stage in this chapter.

In Table 5.8, we shall highlight the total area of land acquired by sample households from other sources including land from land reform measures. The total land received through various sources by 26 households from 3 districts *viz*. Ahmedabad, Mehsana and Surendranagar was 75.27 hectares. The district of Kaira had no household with land acquired from sources other than heredity. Going back to Table 5.8 we find that there were 18 households in the district of Kaira who inherited 18.58 hectares of land. The land received by inheritance in other 3 districts was quite substantial in comparison to the land received through other sources.

We have presented under major 3 sub-divisions the analysis of land received by 26 households form various sources other than heredity. There were 17 households who received a total of 48.38 hectares of land not only under land reforms acts, but also under other government schemes, such as distribution of wasteland, fallow land and village pasture land. The cases of distribution of land to landless labourers from the pasture land (or village green) were not reported significantly in the present data. But it is likely that landless labourers elsewhere might have been benefitted from this category of land. In any case, we shall present further analysis of the 17 households who received land generally on account of land reforms and other government schemes. It is important to note from Table 5.8 that there were 5 households who received 15.66 hectares of land under Bhoodan movement and there were 4 households who purchased 11.23 hectares of land from others in the village.

The detailed analysis of 17 households who were recipients of land under land reforms and other government shcemes is presented in Table

TABLE 5.8 Area of Land Received from Govt. and Other Sources

District	No. of H.H.	Total land received (Hect.)	No. of H.H.	Total land received under Govt. schemes (Hect.)	No. of H.H.	Total land received under Bhoodan (Hect.)	No. of H.H.	Total land purchased from others (Hect.)
Ahmedabad	10	26.64	8	20.31	—	—	2	6.33
Kaira	—	—	—	—	—	—	—	—
Mehsana	4	5.15	4	5.15	—	—	—	—
Surendranagar	12	43.48	5	22.92	5	15.66	2	4.90
Total	26	75.27	17	48.38	5	15.66	4	11.23

TABLE 5.9 Households Receiving Land Through Land Reforms and Other Schemes

District	Different sources of land acquisition									
	Recepients of Govt. land		Under Land Ceiling Act		Govt. Waste Land		Under other Govt. Schemes		Under Jagir Abolition Act.	
	No. of H.H.	Area (Hect.)	NO. of H.H.	Area (Hect.)	No.of H.H.	Area (Hect.)	No. of H.H.	Area (Hect.)	No. of H.H.	Area (Hect.)
Ahmedabad	8	20.31	1	3.45	3	4.80	4	12.06	—	—
Kaira	—	—	—	—	—	—	—	—	—	—
Mehsana	4	5.15	3	3.95	—	—	—	—	1	1.20
Surendranagar	5	22.92	3	15.60	2	7.32	—	—	—	—
Total	17	48.38	7	23.00	5	12.12	4	12.06	1	1.20

5.9. The total area of land so received by the 17 households comes to be 48.38 hectares. Seven households from this group received 23.0 hectares of land under Land Ceiling Act, 5 households received 12.12 hectares of land from government waste, 4 households received 12.06 hectares of land under other schemes and only one household received 1.20 hectares of land under Jagirdari Abolition Act. It was interesting to note that 7 households who received land under Land Ceiling Act, came from the districts of Ahmedabad, Mehsana and Surendranagar, while 5 households who received government waste land came from the districts of Ahmedabad and Surendranagar. The recipients of land under other government schemes came from Ahmedabad while the one receiving land under Jagirdari Abolition Act came from the district of Mehsana.

Landholders With or Without Income from Land

In this section, we shall throw light on the potentiality or otherwise of the landholders with respect to the income that accrued to them from the land under their possession. Those who received income from land were 88 households out of 105. Table 5.10 gives details of the number of households of all the 4 sample districts who were fortunate in getting income from agricultural landholdings. Land holdings of 26 households from Ahmedabad district amounted to 58.75 hectares and they formed 86.67 per cent of the total number of households from the district. From the district of Kaira, there were 17 households owning 18.36 hectares of land. In the district of Mehsana, there were 21 households owning 44.71

TABLE 5.10: Households With and Without Income from Land

District	Total land-holders		Receiving income from land		Not receiving income from land	
	No. of H.H.	Land in Hect.	No. of H.H.	Land in Hect.	No. of H.H.	Land in Hect.
Ahmedabad	30 100.00	65.56	26	58.75 86.67	4	6.81 13.33
Kaira	18 100.00	18.55	17	18.36 94.44	1	0.19 5.56
Mehsana	25 100.00	49.86	21	44.71 84.00	4	5.15 16.00
Surendranagar	32 100.00	146.28	24	116.75 75.00	8	29.53 25.00
Total	105 100.00	280.25	88	238.57 83.81	17	41.68 16.19

hectares of land and in Surendranagar there were 24 households having 116.75 hectares of land from which agricultural income was available. The number of households not receiving any income from land under their possession were in all 17 and the total area amounted to 41.68 hectares of land. The district wise details are available from the table. However, it is interesting to note that the district of Surendranagar had 75.00 per cent of households receiving income from land, while 25.00 per cent were those who did not receive any income from land. This kind of difference was not found in the case of other 3 districts. One of the explanations of this unique phenomenon is that the Bhoodan movement in Gujarat was initiated from the district of Surendranagar and it is likely that number of scheduled castes people who received land were in possession of almost unproductive land usually received through the source of Bhoodan.

We shall now throw some light on the distribution of sample households who were able to get income from land received through different sources. We, therefore, give the break-up of 88 households in possession of 238.57 hectares of land in Table 5.11. In the first category of landholders fall those who were in possession of hereditary land. Secondly, there were 75 households in posession of 192.50 hectares of land. There were 10 households who received land under Land Reform Acts and other government schemes.

These households were in possession of 31.39 hectares of land. There was only one household receiving 3.45 hectares of land from Bhoodan and this household came from the district of Surendranagar. It is significant to note that there were only 4 households who were able to purchase land from others in the village. Two of these households came from Ahmedabad and were in possession of 6.33 hectares of land. The other 2 came from the district of Surendranagar and were in possession of 4.98 hectares of land.

Table 5.12 throws light on the reasons why the 17 households in possession of land were not able to get any income. In the case of landholders, who received land by inheritance, we have 4 households with 5.89 hectares of land mortgaged to the money-lenders. This shows that the money-lender was virtually in possession of all the produce of the land under mortgage. In this category, there were 2 households with 6.59 hectares of land which was kept fallow. It means that these people were not reaping any harvest from the land in their possession during the period of investigation. In the case of those who received land under land reforms and government schemes, there was one household who had mortgaged 1.15 hectares of land under its possession. In the same category, there were 6 households in possession of 15.84 hectares of land who did not get any

TABLE 5.11 Households with Size of Land Economic Units of Land from Different Sources

District	No. of H.H.	Total Land (Hect.)	Hereditory		Under land Reforms and Govt. Schemes		Under Bhoodan		Land by purchase	
			No. of H.H.	Area (Hect.)	No. of H.H.	Area (Hect.)	No. of H.H.	Area (Hect.)	No. of H.H.	Area (Hect.)
Ahmedabad	26	58.75	17	34.23	7	18.19	—	—	2	6.33
Kaira	17	18.36	17	18.36	—	—	—	—	—	—
Mehsana	21	44.71	20	43.51	1	1.20	—	—	—	—
Surendranagar	24	116.75	19	96.40	2	12.00	1	3.45	2	4.90
Total	88	238.57	73	192.50	10	31.39	1	3.45	4	11.23

TABLE 5.12: Area of Non-remunerative Land from Different Sources

District	Total land area giving no income		Hereditary land				By land reforms				Bhoodan land			
			Under Mortage		Fallow land		Under Mortgage		Fallow Land		Under Mortagage		Fallow Land.	
	No. of HH	Area (Hect.)	No.of HH	Area (Hect.)	No.of HH	Area (Hect.)	No.of HH	Area (Hect.)	No.of HH	Area (Hect.)	No.of HH	Area (Hect.)	No.of HH	Area in (Hect.)
Ahmedabad	4	6.81	3	4.69	—	—	—	—	1	2.12	—	—	—	—
Kaira	1	0.19	—	—	1	0.19	—	—	—	—	—	—	—	—
Mehasana	4	5.15	1	1.20	—	—	1	1.15	2	2.80	—	—	—	—
Surendranagar	8	29.53	—	—	1	6.40	—	—	3	10.92	—	—	4	12.2
Total	17	41.68	4	5.89	2	6.59	1	1.15	6	15.84	—	—	4	12.21

income becuase they kept the land fallow. In the 3rd category of land, from which no income was received, was Bhoodan land. Out of the 4 households receiving land from Bhoodan there was none who mortagaged land to a money-lender. This means that all of them kept their land fallow and here the reasons of keeping the land fallow and not getting any income was likely to be associated with the lack of fertility of Bhoodan land.

Income from Land Held by Households

In this sub-section, we come back to consider the position of all the 88 households who were owners of land in order to make an assessment of the tangible income received by them. In Table 5.13 are presented the data on income of households received annually from agricultural land.

This is based on the broad classification of land received from ancestors under land reforms, Bhoodan and private purchases by the households in recent times. It is significant to note that there were 22 households from the district of Mehsana and 19 from the district of Surendranagar who received income from land inherited by them. Surprisingly, the income per household in both these cases was around Rs. 3,500 per household. Similarly, from the districts of Ahmedabad and Kaira, there were 17 households each with average income of around Rs. 2,500. The total income of all the 73 households, who inherited land, amounted to Rs. 2,21,824. This was the highest score with regard to landholding and income received by the land owning scheduled castes households under study. The remaining households were only 15 of which 10 received land under land reform acts with the total annual income of Rs. 8,541. There was only one case receiving land under Bhoodan with the total income of Rs. 157 only. There were remaining 4 households who purchased land recently and were able to get the total income of Rs. 8,951. This was quite high in comparision to income of 10 households who received land under land reforms. The total income from them was only Rs. 8,541 as indicated earlier. This amounted to say that the scheduled castes landholders receiving land on account of land reforms did not receive substantial income possibly because of poorer quality of land.

In Table 5.14 is presented data on per capita income received by land owning households from agriculture. This is assessed annually and in context of different sources from which land was received by them. The number of members of the 88 households with land as a source of income was 617. Their total income was Rs. 2,39,467 and income per capita came to be Rs. 388. As per Table 5.13 referred to earlier, the income of members of households who received land by inheritance is substantially high in

TABLE 5.13 Annual Income per Household from Land

District	H.H.			By Inheritance			Under land reforms Acts			Under Bhoodan			By purchase		
	No. of H.H.	Total Income Rs.	Income per H.H. Rs.	No. of H.H.	Total Income Rs.	Income per H.H. Rs.	No. of H.H.	Total Income Rs.	Income per H.H. Rs.	No. of H.H.	Total Income Rs.	Income per H.H. Rs.	No. of H.H.	Total Income Rs.	Income per H.H. Rs.
Ahmedabad	26	50365	1937	17	41714	2454	7	3822	545	—	—	—	2	4829	2414
Kaira	17	46529	2737	17	46529	2737	—	—	—	—	—	—	—	—	—
Mehsana	21	66161	3151	20	65881	3294	1	280	280	—	—	—	—	—	—
Surendranagar	24	76412	3184	19	67700	3563	2	4439	2219	1	151	151	2	4122	2061
Total	88	239467	2721	73	221824	3039	10	8541	854	1	151	151	4	8951	2238

TABLE 5.14 Per Capita Annual Income from Land

District	Total No.of Members	Total agricultural Income		Income from hereditary land			Income from land under reforms			Income from land under Bhoodan			Income from land by purchase		
		Total Income Rs.	Per Capita Income Rs.	No.of Members	Total Income Rs.	Per Capita Income Rs.	No.of Members	Total Income Rs.	Per Capita Income Rs.	N.of Mem-bers	Total Income Rs.	Per Capita Income Rs.	No.of Mem-bers	Total Income Rs.	Per Capita Income Rs.
Ahmedabad	189	50365	266	129	41714	323	46	3822	83	—	—	—	14	4829	345
Kaira	89	46529	523	89	46529	523	—	—	—	—	—	—	—	—	—
Mehsana	193	66161	343	181	65881	364	12	280	23	-	-	-	—	—	—
Surendranagar	146	76412	523	118	67700	574	7	4439	634	9	151	17	12	4122	343
Total	617	239467	388	517	221824	429	65	8541	131	9	151	17	26	8951	344

relation to those who received land from other sources. It is significant to note that the per capita income of landholders who received land by inheritance was considerably high in the districts of Kaira and Surendranagar. The same was relatively low in the districts of Ahmedabad and Mehsana. This phenomenon appeared to be reasonable to happen because the quality of smaller size of agricultural land from Kaira was relatively richer and the overall size of landholdings in the case of Surendranagar was relatively higher.

The income per capita, received under land reforms in Ahmedabad, was Rs. 83, from Mehsana Rs. 23 and from Surendranagar Rs.634. Here the difference of per capita income from Surendranagar district receiving land under land reforms was very high. The only reason why such a great difference in income per capita appeared from this category of land received, may be that the land received by the 2 households with 7 members was quite fertile. In the case of 4 households with the total of 26 members who purchased land, the per capita income came to be Rs. 344. This was quite nearer to the per capita income received by households with ancestral land. The overall per capita income received by households from land reforms and Bhoodan was found to be relatively low and poor, respectively.

We shall now deal with the information regarding net income received per hectare from agricultural land. See Table 5.15. This subject is also treated in terms of land received by inheritance under land reforms, under Bhoodan and purchased by the households concerned. The overall position indicates that the net income from the total of 238.57 hectares of land from all the sample households of 4 districts comes to be Rs. 2,39,467. This means that the income per hectare came to be Rs. 1004. While comparing the over all situation of income per hectare with land received from different sources, we come across interesting results. In the case of land received by inheritance, we have 192.50 hectares of land giving net income of Rs. 2,21,824. Here the income per capita came to be Rs. 1152, which was considerably high in relation to the over all per hectare income. When we come to consider 31.39 hectares of land received under land reforms, we find that net income came to be Rs. 8,541, while per capita income came to be Rs. 272. In relation to the size of land held under this category, the per capita income was extremely low. In the case of land purchased by the household, the total area was 11.23 hectares from which net income received was Rs. 8,951 and income per capita came to be Rs. 797. While comparing this with the total land and per capita income of landholders, receiving land from land reforms, the position of those who had themselves purchased land, was far better. It is needless to say

TABLE 5.15 Net Annual Income Per Hectare of Land

District	Consolidated position			By Inheritance			Under land-Reforms			Under Bhoodan			By purchase		
	Total land in Hectare	Net Income Rs.	Income per (Hec.) Rs.	Total land (Hect.)	Net Income Rs.	Income per Capita Rs.	Total land (Hect.)	Net Income Rs.	Income per Capita Rs.	Total land (Hect.)	Net Income Rs.	Income per Capita Rs.	Total land (Hect.)	Net Income Rs.	Income per Capita Rs.
Ahmedabad	58.75	50365	857	34.23	41714	1219	18.19	3822	210	—	—	—	6.33	4829	763
Kaira	18.36	46529	2534	18.36	46529	2534	—	—	—	—	—	—	—	—	—
Mehsana	44.71	66121	1479	43.51	65881	1514	1.20	280	233	—	—	—	—	—	—
Surendranagar	116.75	76412	654	96.40	67700	702	12.00	4439	369	3.45	151	44	4.90	4122	841
Total	238.57	239467	1004	192.50	221824	1152	31.39	8541	272	3.45	151	44	11.23	8951	797

TABLE 5.16 Remunarative and Non-remunarative Landholdings

Sources of land acquisition	Total landholders and area		Households having remunerative landholdings and total area		Households having non-remunerative land holdings and total area	
	No. of H.H.	Area in (Hect.)	No. of H.H.	Area in (Hect.)	No. of H.H.	Area in (Hect.)
By Inheritance	79	204.98	73	192.50	6	12.48
Under Land Ceiling Act	7	23.00	3	15.45	4	7.55
Government Waste	5	12.12	3	4.80	2	7.32
Land Reforms	4	12.06	3	9.94	1	2.12
Jagir Abolition Act	1	1.20	1	1.20	—	—
Bhoodan	5	15.66	1	3.45	4	12.21
By Purchase	4	11.23	4	11.23	—	—
Total	105	280.25	88	238.57	17	42.68
	100.00		83.81		16.19	

that the size of land and per capita income from land received under Bhoodan was extremely poor.

In Table 5.16, we have tried to present the general picture of remunerative and non-remunerative landholdings of the households who received land from different sources. This is a recapitulation of the total picture regarding viability or non-viability of landholdings under the possession of scheduled castes households. Those having remunerative landholdings were 83.81 per cent and those with non-remunerative ladholdings were 16.19 per cent of the 105 households.

Members Engaged in Self-Cultivation

In the earlier sections, we discussed the problems of distribution and sources of land, economic viability of land, ownership of land from various sources and income received from the same. In this section, we shall throw light on the number of household members engaged in self-cultivation. We shall throw light also on the assets and necessities required for making agricultural activities remunerative.

In Table 5.17, we have data on the distribution of members of households engaged in agriculture. The totals at the end of the table do not tally because of overlapping categories. The overall picture of scheduled castes engaged in agricultural work indicates that it was just not possible for them to depend on agriculture alone for living. The Table shows that 23 members of both sexes were distributed in the whole group of 105 households with land. As reported earlier, 88 households were receiving income from agriculture. In fact, there were only 8 households who reported agriculture to be their main occupation. In any, case, it was significant to note that out of 23 members, who were directly involved in

TABLE 5.17 Members of Households Engaged in Agriculture

District	Total persons doing Self-cultivation			Age group of members engaged in agriculture								
				15 — 29			30 — 44			45 — 59		
	M	F	Total	M	F	Total	M	F	Total	M	F	Total
Ahmedabad	4	1	5	2	-	2	1	1	2	1	—	1
Kaira	6	2	8	2	1	3	3	1	4	1	—	1
Mehsana	2	1	3	1	-	1	1	1	2	—	—	—
Surendranagar	6	1	7	2	-	2	3	1	4	1	—	1
Total	18	5	23	7	1	8	8	4	12	3	—	3

* *The total figures do not tally because of overlapping categories*

agricultural operations, there were 12 persons including males and females in the age group of 30 to 44. In the younger age group of 6 to 14 years, there were only 7 members and of 15 to 29, only 8 members. This means that only the people of the middle age group among the scheduled castes were able to devote full time for agriculture. This does not mean that they were not assisted by other members of the family at different points of time.

Table 5.18 provides data on ownership of basic facilities available with the landholders. While we consider the ownership of bullocks most essential in agriclture, we find that 31.43 per cent of the households maintained their own bullocks. The same percentage of households were in possession of other minor facilities also. The other essential assets to a cultivator are bullock-carts which were owned by 13.33 per cent of the households under consideration. With regard to facility of field well, diesel oil pumping set, tube well, hand pump, etc., the percentages of households having these facilities came to be 6.67, 4.76, and 0.95, respectively.

In Table 5.19, we have the break-up of number of bullocks owned by 33 households referred to in the previous table. There were in all 19 households with one, 10 with two, 2 with three and four bullocks, respectively.

With regard to ownership of essential minor facilities *viz.* tools and equipments, we found that 14 (13.3%) of the households out of 105 had sufficient number of these facilieties essential in conducting agricultural operations. There were 19 (18.10%) of the households who did not have all the minor facilities at their disposal. It was natural that these families borrowed minor tools from others for their farming activities. The percentage of households without facilities for doing independent farming came to be 72 (68.57%). This indicated that quite a number of them either mortaged their land or kept fallow on account of poverty and were therefore unable to acquire the necessary assets for cultivation.

There were 76 (72.38%) of the households without irrigation facilities while 29 (27.62%) were able to get these facilities. Of the 29 households who had irrigation facilities for cultivation, 5 households were able to use irrigation water in 11.71 hectares of land from their own field wells. There were 18 households who irrigated 15.34 hectares of land by water received from others' wells. There were 5 households using irrigation water from government canal system for 5.68 hectares of land. In the end, there was only one household irrigating 2.00 hectares of land from tube-well.

TABLE 5.18 Ownership of Farming Facilities by Households

District	No. of Households	A pair of bullocks HH	Cart	Other minor facilities HH	Field work tools HH	Oil engine for lift irrigation HH	Tubewell HH	Hand pump HH	Pump for insecticide HH
Ahmedabad	30	11 (36.67)	8 (26.67)	11 (36.67)	5 (16.67)	3 (10.0)	—	1 (3.33)	1 (3.33)
Kaira	18	4 (22.22)	2 (11.11)	4 (22.22)	—	—	—	—	—
Mehsana	25	8 (32.00)	1 (4.00)	9 (36.00)	—	—	—	—	—
Surendranagar	32	10 (31.25)	3 (9.38)	10 (31.25)	2 (6.25)	2 (6.25)	1 (3.13)	—	—
Total	105	33 (31.43)	14 (13.33)	33 (31.43)	7 (6.76)	5 (4.76)	1 (0.95)	1 (0.95)	1 (0.95)

TABLE 5.19 Households Owning Bullocks

District	No. of H.H.	House-holds with out bullocks	House-holds with bullocks	No. of bullocks owned			
				1	2	3	4
Ahmedabad	30	19 (63.33)	11 (36.67)	7 (63.64)	3 (27.27)	—	1 (9.09)
Kaira	18	14 (77.78)	4 (22.22)	1 (25.00)	3 (75.00)	—	—
Mehsana	25	17 (68.00)	8 (32.00)	6 (75.00)	2 (25.00)	—	—
Surendranagar	32	22 (68.75)	10 (31.25)	5 (50.00)	2 (20.00)	2 (20.00)	1 (10.00)
Total	105	72 (68.57)	33 (31.43)	19 (57.58)	10 (30.30)	2 (86.06)	2 (6.06)

6

CROPPING PATTERN, INPUTS AND NEW TECHNOLOGY

Introduction

In the preceding chapter we have presented detailed analysis of landholdings of the sample households of scheduled castes. The analysis has thrown light on the distribution of land among different groups of scheduled castes, hereditary and non-hereditary sources of land, ones ability to get income or otherwise from agriculture according to the nature of land acquired and received under land reforms acts or Bhoodan movement. It also gave a general idea of the income received by households of various categories in terms of the area of land in hectares in their possession.

In this chapter, we shall deal with the data throwing light on the cropping pattern followed by landholding households. We shall also cover information on the intensity of cropping, position regarding the cultivation of mortgaged or fallow land, area under irrigation in terms of size of plot and the variety of crops both staple and commercial

In the next section of this chapter, we shall deal with area under irrigation or otherwise, specially as related to the use of fertilisers, insecticides and improved seeds, mechanisation of operations for improvement of yield from land.

In the third section of this chapter, detailed information is given on the distribution of members of landholding households by age and sex. Apart from this information and general aspects of landholdings, we shall throw light on other important aspects with respect to income received from agriculture not only district-wise but also in relation to the sub-castes of scheduled castes. Since the landholdings of most of the sample households were not adequate for the maintenance of family members, they had no alternative but to do other occupations. We have, therefore, tried to provide data on subsidiary occupations followed by marginal, small, medium and big landholders among the scheduled castes.

Cropping Pattern

Before we present data on cropping pattern, it will be useful to know the extent of area under cultivation and where cultivation has not been possible due to land being mortgaged or kept fallow by the landholders. Table 6.1 shows that out of total 280.25 hectares of land, held by 105 households, the area under cultivation was 17.84 per cent in Ahmedabad, 6.55 per cent in Kaira, 15.35 per cent in Mehsana and 36.81 per cent in Surendranagar. The overall percentage area under cultivation came to be 76.56 per cent of the total landholdings. The land, which was not mortgaged or kept fallow, was 65.80 hectares. The overall mortgaged land of the total landholdings came to be 6.47 per cent, while the extent of land kept fallow came to be 16.97 per cent.

TABLE 6.1 Cultivated and Non-cultivated Area of Land

District	Total area of land with Households Hect.	Area under Cultivation Hect.	Non-cultivated area: Mortgaged land Hect.	Non-cultivated area: Fallow land Hect.
Ahmedabad	65.56 (23.39)	49.99 (17.84)	7.71 (2.75)	7.86 (2.80)
Kaira	18.55 (6.62)	18.36 (6.55)	— —	0.19 (0.07)
Mehsana	49.86 (17.79)	43.04 (15.35)	4.02 (1.43)	2.80 (1.00)
Surendranagar	146.28 (52.20)	103.16 (36.81)	6.40 (2.28)	36.72 (13.10)
Total	280.25 (100.00)	214.55 (76.56)	18.13 (6.47)	47.57 (16.97)

In Table 6.2, we have presented the data on classification of 242.77 hectares of cultivated land in relation to the coverage by single crop and double crop area in hectares. It may be noted that the single crop area was 214.55 hectares which amounted to 88.38 per cent and double crop area came to be 28.22 hectares, amounting to 11.62 per cent of the total area under cultivation. It is significant to note that of the total area of double crop in the district of Ahmedabad was 6.85 per cent while that in the district of Mehsana was 3.28 per cent only. The districts of Kaira and

Surendranagar had negligible land under double crop cultivation.

TABLE 6.2 Cultivated Area of Land Under Single and Double Crop Pattern

District	Area under cultivation (Hect.)	Single Crop area (Hect.)	Double Crop area (Hect.)
Ahmedabad	66.62 (27.44)	49.98 (20.59)	16.64 (6.85)
Kaira	20.17 (8.31)	18.36 (7.56)	1.81 (0.75)
Mehsana	51.00 (21.01)	43.04 (17.73)	7.96 (3.28)
Surendranagar	103.98 (43.24)	103.16 (42.49)	1.82 (0.75)
Total	242.77 (100.00)	214.55 (88.38)	28.22 (11.62)

In Table 6.3, we shall present data on cultivated and un-cultivated land by area and the number of households owning land. Out of 105 such households, 17 had 41.68 hectares of uncultivated land while 88 households had 238.57 hectares of land under cultivation. Most of the land that was not cultivated was either mortgaged or remained fallow. In the group of cultivated area, we have instances of partially cultivated land. There were 5 households with 4.69 hectares land partially cultivated because of land being mortgaged. There were 8 households with 19.33 hectares of fallow land at times cultivated and, therefore, may be included in the category of partially cultivated area totaling 24.02 hectares.

Now we shall throw light on irrigated and unirrigated area of land in all the 4 sample districts. This was presented in Table 6.4. In relation to food crops and cash crops, the total area of land under irrigation was 34.73 hectares and the area not irrigated amounted to 208.04 hectares. In these 2 categories, land with necessary water input in the district of Surendranagar came on the top with 13.01 hectares. The district of Ahmedabad in the category of irrigated land area came next with 9.65 hectares of land. The districts of Kaira and Mehsana, where canal and tubewell irrigation facilities were generally available to farmers, we had relatively few households with irrigated land as can be seen from the table. It also shows that relatively more unirrigated area of 117.17 hectares was under food crops while considerably smaller unirrigated areas of 90.87 hectares was under cash crops. The picture of different types of food crops and the area under irrigated and unirrigated categories are presented in Table 6.5. Looking at the total picture of different types of food crops, we

TABLE 6.3 Size of Mortgaged and Fallow Land Cultivated or Otherwise

District	No. of H.H.	Area of Land in Hect.	H.H. and area of uncultivated land				H.H. with uncultivated land		H.H. with cultivated land		H.H. with partially cultivated area				Partially cultivated area & HH.	
			All land mortgaged		All land kept fallow						Mortgaged		Fallow			
			No. of H.H.	Area of land (Hect.)	No. of H.H.	Area of land (Hect.)	No. of H.H.	Area of land (Hect.)	No. of HH	Area of land (Hect.)	No. of HH	Area (Hect.)	No. of HH	Area (Hect.)	No. of H.H.	Area of land (Hect.)
Ahmedabad	30	65.56	3	4.69	1	2.12	4	6.81	26	58.75	3	3.02	2	5.74	5	8.76
Kaira	18	18.55	2	2.35	1	0.19	3	0.19	17	18.36	2	1.67	—	—	2	1.67
Mehsana	25	49.86	—	—	2	2.80	2	5.15	21	44.71	—	—	—	—	—	—
Surendranagar	32	146.28	1	6.40	7	23.13	8	29.53	24	116.75	—	—	6	13.59	6	13.59
Total	105	280.25	6	13.44	11	28.24	17	41.68	88	238.57	5	4.69	8	19.33	13	24.02

TABLE 6.4 Irrigated and Non-irrigated Areas of Land

Broad classes of crops	Ahmedabad			Kaira			Mehsana			Surendranagar			Total		
	Irrigated (Hect.)	Non-Irrigated (Hect.)	Total	Irrigated (Hect.)	Non-Irrigated (Hect.)	Total	Irrigated (Hect.)	Non-Irrigated (Hect.)	Total	Irrigated (Hect.)	Non-Irrigated (Hect.)	Total	Irrigated (Hect.)	Non-Irrigated (Hect.)	Total
Food crops	9.65	46.00	55.65	3.65	13.06	16.71	5.44	16.67	22.11	4.81	41.44	46.25	23.55	117.17	140.72
Cash crops	—	10.97	10.97	0.46	3.00	3.46	2.52	26.37	28.89	8.20	50.53	58.73	11.18	90.87	102.05
Total	9.65	56.97	66.62	4.11	16.06	20.17	7.96	43.04	51.00	13.01	91.97	104.98	34.73	208.04	242.77

TABLE 6.5 Irrigated and Unirrigated Land Under Food Crops

Name of Crops	Ahmedabad			Kaira			Mehsana			Surendranagar			Total		
	Irri-gated (Hect.)	Unirri-gated (Hect.)	Total	Irri-gated (Hect.)	Unirri-gated (Hect.)	Total	Irri-gated (Hect.)	Unirri-gated (Hect.)	Total	Irri-gated (Hect.)	Unirri-gated (Hect.)	Total	Irri-gated (Hect.)	Unirri-gated (Hect.)	Total
Bajra	1.76	29.35	31.11	2.87	9.19	12.06	1.75	7.20	8.95	1.95	23.63	25.58	8.33	69.37	77.70
Wheat	6.04	3.10	9.14	0.04	1.38	1.42	2.49	3.35	5.84	1.71	6.80	8.51	10.28	14.63	24.91
Juwar	1.65	5.42	7.07	—	—	—	—	3.03	3.03	1.15	11.01	12.16	2.80	19.46	22.26
Paddy	—	4.41	4.41	—	1.42	1.42	—	—	—	—	—	—	—	5.83	5.83
Tuver Dal	—	1.84	1.84	0.74	—	0.74	—	—	—	—	—	—	0.74	1.84	2.58
Horse-gram	—	—	—	—	—	—	—	2.29	2.29	—	—	—	—	2.29	2.29
Green-gram Mag	0.20	—	0.20	—	—	—	—	0.80	0.80	—	—	—	0.20	0.80	1.00
Guvar	—	1.88	1.88	—	—	—	—	—	—	—	—	—	—	1.88	1.88
Sugar-cane	—	—	—	—	1.07	1.07	—	—	—	—	—	—	—	1.07	1.07
Banti	—	—	—	—	—	—	1.20	—	1.20	—	—	—	1.20	—	1.20
Total	9.65	46.00	55.65	3.65	13.06	16.71	5.44	16.67	22.11	4.81	41.11	46.25	23.55	117.17	140.72

find that Bajari, Wheat and Jawar stand out to be the main crops. Most of these 3 types of crops are taken without irrigation facilities. Among the irrigated area, wheat stands out first and it was followed by Bajari, Jawar and Banti for which irrigation facilities were available. Out of the total of 23.55 hectares of irrigated land, 9.65 hectares were from Ahmedabad, 5.44 hectares from Mehsana, 4.81 hectares from Surendranagar and 3.65 hectares from Kaira.

So far as availability of irrigation facilities for cash crops is concerned, we have data in Table 6.6. It is evident that the total area under cash crops was relatively less than that under food crops. Overall picture of cash crops indicates that 11.18 hectares were under irrigation and 90.87 hectares without irrigation. In the irrigated variety, cotton was grown in 8.60 hectares of land. The next important crop in this category was, of course, grain Raido in 2.12 hectares of land. It is interesting to note that cotton was grown by scheduled castes in relatively more area in the district of Surendranagar amounting to 50.81 hectares of land. The next district where cotton was grown was Mehsana, where 21.62 hectares of land was covered. The next important cash crop was Tal, oilseeds, which covered the total area of 11.64 hectares of land. It was cultivated only in the district of Surendranagar and Ahmedabad with the coverage of 7.70 hectares and 3.94 hectares of land respectively.

The crops of Raido, caster, tobacco and Jiru come next in importance to the earlier two crops. Here, we find that 3.0 hectares of land was covered under tobacco in the district of Kaira only. The cash crop of Raido and caster were more prominently sown in the districts of Ahmedabad and Mehsana. The overall picture indicated that the scheduled castes people were not able to take advantage of covering more land under these cash crops.

We shall present in Table 6.7 a consolidated picture of area of land under food crops and cash crops alongwith the income thereof. The total income from the food crops covering 140.72 hectares of land came to be Rs. 2,16,101. In relation to this, the area of land under cash crops was 102.05 hectares of land and the total income was Rs. 1,94,674. This shows that relatively the cash crops were more remunerative than the food crops for which relatively more area was covered. When we look at the district-wise picture of number of households taking advantage of food and cash crops, we find that in Ahmedabad there were 45 households taking food crops and 9 households cash crops. In the district of Surendranagar the proportion of households taking food crops and cash crops was almost equal while in the district of Mehsana the proportion of households taking food and cash crops was not so different as in the case of both Ahmedabad

TABLE 6.6 Irrigated and Non-irrigated Land Under Cash Crops

Name of Crops	Ahmedabad			Kaira			Mehsana			Surendranagar			Total		
	Irri-gated (Hect.)	Unirri-gated (Hect.)	Total	Irri-gated (Hect.)	Unirri-gated (Hect.)	Total	Irri-gated (Hect.)	Unirri-gated (Hect.)	Total	Irri-gated (Hect.)	Unirri-gated (Hect.)	Total	Irri-gated (Hect.)	Unirri-gated (Hect.)	Total
Cotton	—	43.56	43.56	—	—	—	0.40	21.22	21.62	8.20	42.61	50.81	8.60	68.39	76.99
Tal	—	3.94	3.94	—	—	—	—	—	—	—	7.70	7.70	—	11.64	11.64
Raido	—	1.15	1.15	—	—	—	2.12	1.15	3.67	1.15	—	1.15	2.12	2.70	4.82
Castor	—	1.32	1.32	—	—	—	1.30	—	1.30	—	0.22	0.22	—	2.84	2.84
Tobaco	—	—	—	—	3.00	3.00	—	—	—	—	—	—	—	3.00	3.00
Mustard and Variari	—	—	—	0.46	—	0.46	—	0.60	0.60	—	—	—	0.46	0.60	1.06
Chasara and Jiru	—	—	—	—	—	—	—	1.70	1.70	—	—	—	—	1.70	1.70
Total	—	10.97	10.97	0.46	3.00	3.46	2.52	26.37	28.89	8.20	50.53	58.73	11.18	90.87	102.05

TABLE 6.7 Area of Land With Value of Food and Cash Crops

Types of Crops	Ahmedabad				Kaira				Mehsana				Surendranagar				Total for all Districts			
	No.of H.H.	Area in Hect.	Value of yield		No.of H.H.	Area (Hect.)	Value of yield		No.of H.H.	Area (Hect.)	Value of yield		No. of H.H.	Area (Hect.)	Value of yield		No.of H.H.	Area (Hect.)	Value of yield	
			Total Rs.	Hect. Rs.			Total Rs.	Hect. Rs.			Total Rs.	Hect. Rs.			Total Rs.	Hect. Rs.			Total Rs.	Hect. Rs
Food-Crops	45	55.65	81498	1464	21	16.71	44008	2488	30	22.11	58045	2625	27	46.25	32500	703	123	140.72	216101	1536
Cash-Crops	9	10.97	12300	1121	7	3.46	17590	7150	19	28.89	50414	1745	25	58.73	114370	1947	60	102.05	194674	1908
Total	54	66.62	93798	1478	28	20.17	61648	3056	49	51.00	108459	2127	52	104.98	146870	1399	183	242.77	410775	1692

and Kaira. In terms of value of yield per hectare, we find that the scheduled castes in Ahmedabad and Surendranagar got around Rs. 1,400 from both types of crops. The income per hectare in the district of Kaira was the highest and it to be Rs. 3,056. The district of Mehsana stood next in this respect and its income per hectare from both the kinds of crops came to be Rs. 2,127.

In Table 6.8, we shall throw light on cropwise area of land and value of different kinds of food crops. The total number of households taking food crops was 123. They cover 140.72 hectares of land from which the total income came to be Rs. 2,16,101. The income per hectare of land from food crops amounted to be Rs. 1,536. When we compare this average income per hectare for all the four sample districts collectively, we find that the scheduled castes households in the districts of Kaira and Mehsana were able to get more income per hectare of land from food crops. The total picture with regard to different types of crops shows that bajari, wheat and jawar were cultivated in larger area of land and were able to get better income than from other crops. There were, however, other crops with less coverage of land, but substantially higher income per hectare. It is significant to note that paddy was grown in only 5.83 hectares of land giving the average income of Rs. 5,026 per hectare of land. In the case of horsegram, the land covered was 2.29 hectares for which income per hectare came to be Rs. 3,319. The other important food crops were banti and gavar which are generally used as cattle feed. The income per hectares from banti crop came to be Rs. 4,667, while from gavar it came to be Rs. 1,053, even though the area under cultivation for both these crops was around one hectare of land. As can be seen from the table, the crop of mung and sugarcane got relatively better income per hectare. However, the crop of mung was able to earn the net income of Rs. 1,475.

The data on area of land and value of cash crops have been presented in Table 6.9. As indicated in earlier table, there were 3 important cash crops sown by the scheduled castes farmers in relatively greater areas of land. These crops were cotton, tal, and raido. However, in terms of the value of yield per hectare, we find that mustard, tobacco, chasara and casteroil seeds were able to fetch more income per hectare. the overall income per hectare from all categories of cash crops in the district of Ahmedabad was Rs. 1,121, Kaira Rs. 5,083, Mehsana Rs. 1,745 and Surendranagar Rs. 1,947. It is significant to note that the scheduled castes landholders in the district of Kaira who grew casterd seeds and variali earned average per hectare income of Rs. 5,083. The income from tal and jiru per hectare in relation to all the districts turns out to be very low in Kaira.

TABLE 6.8 Crop Wise Land Area and Value of Food Crops

Types of Crops	Ahmedabad				Kaira				Mehsana				Surendranagar				Total for all Districts			
	No.of H.H.	Area in Hect.	Value of yield		No. of H.H.	Area (Hect.)	Value of yield		No. of H.H.	Area (Hect.)	Value of Yield		No. of H.H.	Area (Hect.)	Value of yield		No. of H.H.	Area (Hect.)	Value of yield	
			Total	Hect.			Total	Hect.			Total	Hect.			Total	Hect.			Total	Hect.
Bajari	20	31.11	27568	886	14	12.06	23258	1929	12	8.95	13270	1483	17	25.58	16475	644	63	77.80	80571	1036
Wheat	12	9.14	24655	2697	2	1.42	3125	2201	8	5.84	24475	4191	4	8.51	4700	552	26	24.91	56955	2286
Juwar	3	7.07	11900	1683	—	—	—	—	4	3.03	6400	2412	6	12.16	11325	931	13	22.26	29625	1331
Paddy	3	4.41	14800	3356	3	1.42	14500	10211	—	—	—	—	—	—	—	—	6	5.83	29300	5026
Tuvar	1	1.84	420	228	1	0.74	700	864	—	—	—	—	—	—	—	—	2	2.65	1120	423
Horse-Gram	—	—	—	—	—	—	—	—	2	2.29	7600	3319	—	—	—	—	2	2.29	7600	3319
Sugar-cane	—	—	—	—	1	1.07	2475	1237	—	—	—	—	—	—	—	—	1	2.00	2475	1237
Mung	1	0.20	175	875	—	—	—	—	3	0.80	1300	1625	—	—	—	—	4	1.00	1475	1475
Guvar	5	1.88	1980	1035	—	—	—	—	—	—	—	—	—	—	—	—	5	1.88	1980	1053
Banti	—	—	—	—	—	—	—	—	1	1.20	5000	4157	—	—	—	—	1	1.20	5000	4167
Total	45	55.65	81498	1464	21	16.71	44058	2488	30	22.11	58045	2625	27	46.25	32500	703	123	140.72	216101	1536

TABLE 6.9 Crop Wise Land Area and Value of Cash Crops

Types of Crops	Ahmedabad				Kaira				Mehsana				Surendranagar				Total for all Districts			
	No.of H.H.	Area in Hect.	Value of yield		No.of H.H.	Area (Hect.)	Value of yield		No.of H.H.	Area (Hect.)	Value of yield		H.H.	Area (Hect.)	Value of yield		No.of H.H.	Area (Hect.)	Value of yield	
			Total	Hect.			Total	Hect.			Total	Hect.			Total	Hect.			Total	Hect.
Cotton	3	4.56	4600	1009	—	—	—	—	11	21.62	38425	1777	21	50.81	110490	2250	35	76.99	153515	1994
Tal.	3	3.94	1280	317	—	—	—	—	—	—	—	—	3	7.70	2980	317	6	11.64	4260	366
Raido	1	1.15	3520	3352	—	—	—	—	2	3.67	4785	1304	—	—	—	—	3	4.82	8315	1725
Castor-seeds	2	1.32	2900	2197	—	—	—	—	3	1.30	2370	1823	1	0.22	900	4091	6	2.84	6170	2173
Tobacco	—	—	—	—	6	3.00	11990	3996	—	—	—	—	—	—	—	—	6	3.00	11990	3996
Mustard seeds	—	—	—	—	—	—	—	—	1	0.60	3200	5333	—	—	—	—	1	0.60	3200	5333
Variari	—	—	—	—	1	0.46	5600	12174	—	—	—	—	—	—	—	—	1	0.46	5600	12174
Chasara	—	—	—	—	—	—	—	—	1	0.50	1250	2500	—	—	—	—	1	0.50	1250	2500
Jiru	—	—	—	—	—	—	—	—	1	1.20	384	320	—	—	—	—	1	1.20	384	320
Total	9	10.97	12300	1121	7	3.46	17590	5083	19	28.89	50414	1745	25	58.73	114370	1947	60	102.05	194674	1907

In Table 6.10, we shall now present consolidated figure of food as well as cash crop yield used by the landholders either for consumption or for sale. The total picture indicates that 1,341.70 quintals of cash crops were produced by the households of scheduled castes under study. Out of this, 383.65 quintals were used for domestic purpose while 958.05 quintals used for sales. It may be noted that some of the food crops were able to fetch as much money as the cash crops because of unique rise in price in most of the commodities of consumption. The picture regarding the cash crops indicated that a total of 452.55 quintals of cash crops were produced by the households. Of this, 4.70 quintals were used for domestic use and 447.85 quintals were sold out in the market. In terms of sales of produce from both types of crops we find that Kaira came first with 417.60 quintals followed by Ahmedabad with 355.10 quintals, Surendranagar 339.00 quintals and Mehsana with 296.20 quintals.

In Table 6.11, we have presented data indicating the amount of food crops consumed by the households and surplus amount sold in the market. The main food crops used for substance were bajari, wheat, jawar and paddy. The total yield of bajari was 517.80 quintals out of which 227.60 quintals were used for consumption. In the same way the amount of wheat produced was 278.00 quintals of which 62.40 quintals were used for consumption. In both these categories of staple food crops, they sold more quintals to earn better income. In the case of paddy also, they produced 174.00 quintals out of which they sold 148.80 quintals and consumed only 25.20 quintals. They consumed more of jawar and sold total of only 98.0 quintals. In the case of Sugarcane, they produced 220 quintals and sold the whole amount for earning cash from the market. This indicates that a food crop in recent times turned out to be as good as cash crop as mentioned earlier.

The district-wise overall picture of consumption and sale shows clearly that the amount of food crops consumed by the households was relatively much less than what was sold by them for earning cash income. In the districts of Kaira and Mehsana, the difference between food crops used for consumption and sale was quite significant. In Ahmedabad the consumption of total amount of food crops was less than 50.00 per cent of the amount sold in the market. In the district of Surendranagar, the differences between the use of food crop for consumption and sale were negligible. The total picture shows that nearly 3 times food crops was sold by the scheduled castes farmers in relation to what they consumed. It seems that the staple food crop of the scheduled castes was jawar which was relatively cheaper than other food crops which they prefer to sell in the market. In all the four districts, the total production of jawar was 98.00

TABLE 6.10 Food Crops and Cash Crop Used for Consumption and Sale

Classificaton of Crops	Ahmedabad			Kaira			Mehsana			Surendranagar			Total for all districts		
	Total yield Quint.	Consu-mption Quint.	Sale Quint.	Total yield Quint.	Consu-mption Quint	Sale Quint.	Total yield Quint.	Consu-mption Quint.	Sale Quint.	Total yield Quint.	Consu-mption Quint.	Sale Quint.	Total yield Quint.	Consu-mption Quint.	Sale Quint.
Food Crops	474.30	153.45	320.85	456.80	73.00	383.80	249.60	82.20	163.40	161.00	75.00	86.00	1341.70	383.65	958.05
Cash Crops	34.75	0.50	34.25	34.00	0.20	33.80	131.80	3.00	128.80	252.00	1.00	251.00	452.55	4.70	447.85
Total	509.05	153.95	355.10	490.80	73.20	417.60	381.40	85.20	296.20	413.00	76.00	337.00	1794.25	388.35	1405.90

TABLE 6.11 Crop Wise Food Crops Used for Consumption and Sale

Name of Crops.	Ahmedabad			Kaira			Mehsana			Surendranagar			Total		
	Total yield Quintal	Consu-mption Quintal	Sale Quintal	Total yield Quintal	Consu-ption Quintal	Sale Quint.	Total yield Quint.	Consu-ption Quint.	Sale Quint.	Total yield Quint.	Consu-ption Quint.	Sale Quint.	Total yield Quintal	Consu-mption Quintal	Sale Quintal.
Bajari	185.40	78.40	107.00	132.80	52.20	80.60	91.60	46.20	45.60	108.20	51.00	57.00	517.80	227.60	290.20
Wheat	138.00	28.00	110.00	25.00	5.40	19.60	91.00	20.00	71.00	24.00	9.00	15.00	278.00	62.40	215.60
Juwar	44.00	36.00	8.00	—	—	—	25.00	10.00	15.00	29.00	15.00	14.00	98.00	61.00	37.00
Paddy	96.00	10.00	86.00	78.00	15.20	62.80	—	—	—	—	—	—	174.00	25.20	148.80
Tuver	1.40	0.20	1.20	1.00	0.20	0.80	—	—	—	—	-	—	2.80	0.40	2.00
House-gram	—	—	—	—	—	—	19.00	2.00	17.00	—	—	—	19.00	2.00	17.00
Sugarcane	—	—	—	220.00	—	220.00	—	—	—	—	—	—	220.00	—	220.00
Mung	0.70	0.05	0.65	—	—	—	3.00	0.20	2.80	—	—	—	3.70	0.25	3.45
Gavar	8.80	0.80	8.00	—	—	—	—	—	—	—	—	—	8.80	0.80	8.00
Banti	—	—	—	—	—	—	20.00	4.00	16.00	—	—	—	20.00	4.00	16.00
Total	474.30	153.45	320.86	456.80	73.00	383.80	242.60	82.20	167.40	161.00	75.00	86.00	1341.70	383.65	958.05

quintals only.

The picture regarding the use of cash crops for consumption and sale is presented in Table 6.12. The comparative figures of food crops and cash crops indicates that in all the four districts, the food crops yield came to be 1341.70 quintals and cash crops 452.55 quintals only. The question of using cash crops for the purpose of consumption did not indicate any favourable results. This is quite natural because a scheduled caste farmer would like to earn cash money from these crops so that it was possible for them to meet other domestic needs to keep the body and soul together. There were cases of 2 cash crops *viz.* variali and chasara, part of which was consumed by the households concerned. Relatively speaking, the use of cash crops for consumption was higher in Surendranagar and Mehsana districts in comparison to the same in Ahmedabad and Kaira.

Use of New Tools and Technology

In this section we shall try to throw light on the use of new tools and technology employed by scheduled castes farmers. We include here a wide rage of innovations which were used for improving farm produce and making cultivation more confortable and helpful. Broadly speaking, right from the use of hybrid seeds, chemical fertilizers, insecticides and irrigation, all innovations used were taken into account while collecting data on the subject.

We present in Table 6.13, the data on number of households with land under irrigation. Out of 105 households owning 280.25 hectares of land, 29 households had only 34.73 hectares of land under irrigation. This indicates that 27.62 per cent of households of scheduled castes were able to irrigate 12.39 hectares of land in their possession.

It is interesting to note that there were 5 households with 13.01 hectares of land under irrigation. In the district of Ahmedabad on the other hand, there were 9 households with 9.65 hectares of land under irrigation. This shows that irrigation facility was available better to scheduled castes farmers in Surendranagar district than in Ahmedabad. The situation regarding number of households and area under irrigation in the districts of Kaira and Mehsana was not outstanding. This is quite surprising because in both these districts, irrigation facilities either through river water canal or tube-well were said to be better placed.

Leaving aside the special character of irrigation water an input, there were a number of other inputs which were easily be used by the farmers. They are insecticides, hybrid variety of seeds, fertilizers, etc. To begin with, we get in Table 6.14, the idea of multiplicity or otherwise of

TABLE 6.12 Crop Wise Cash Crops Used for Consumption and Sale

Name of Crops	Ahmedabad			Kaira			Mehsana			Surendranagar			Total for all districts		
	Total yield Quintal	Consu-mption Quintal	Sale Quintal	Total yield Quintal	Consu-ption Quintal	Sale Quint.	Total yield Quint.	Consu-ption Quint.	Sale Quint.	Total yield Quint.	Consu-ption Quint.	Sale Quint.	Total yield Quintal	Consu-mption Quintal	Sale Quintal.
Cotton	12.50	0.50	12.00	—	—	—	101.00	—	101.00	242.40	1.00	241.40	355.90	1.50	354.40
Tal	2.45	—	2.45	—	—	—	—	—	—	6.60	—	6.60	9.05	—	9.05
Raido	8.80	—	8.80	—	—	—	12.00	12.00	—	—	—	—	20.80	—	20.80
Castor-seeds	11.00	—	11.00	—	—	—	4.20	—	4.20	3.00	—	3.00	18.20	—	18.20
Tobacco	—	—	—	30.00	—	30.00	—	—	—	—	—	—	30.00	—	30.00
Mustard seeds	—	—	—	4.00	0.20	3.80	8.00	—	8.00	—	—	—	12.00	0.20	11.80
Chasara	—	—	—	—	—	—	5.00	3.00	2.00	—	—	—	5.00	3.00	2.00
Jiru	—	—	—	—	—	—	1.60	—	1.60	—	—	—	1.60	—	1.60
Total	34.75	0.50	0.50	34.25	0.20	33.80	131.80	3.00	128.80	252.00	1.00	251.00	452.55	4.70	447.85

TABLE 6.13 Size of Land Under Irrigation

District	No. of H.H.	Total area in Hect.	H.H. and area under irrigation	
			No. of H.H.	Area in Hect.
Ahmedabad	30 (28.57)	65.56	9	9.65
Kaira	18 (17.14)	18.55	8	4.11
Mehsana	25 (23.81)	49.86	7	7.96
Surendranagar	32 (30.48)	146.28	5	13.01
Total	105 (100)	280.25 (100)	29 (27.62)	34.73 (12.39)

the inputs used by the scheduled castes farmers in various combinations. In the district of Ahmedabad, there were 26 households of which 5 reported the use of 3 inputs, 16 of 2 inputs, 3 of one input and 2 were not able to use any agricultural input for improvement of agriculture. In the district of Kaira, there were two households using 3 inputs, 12 using 2 inputs and three using one input.

TABLE 6.14 Households Using Various Combinations of Agricultural Inputs

District	Total No. of H.H.	H.H. using new imputs and technology				
		Multiple inputs etc.	Any three inputs etc.	Any two inputs etc.	Any one inputs etc.	No input
Ahmedabad	26 (29.55)	—	5	16	3	2
Kaira	17 (19.32)	—	2	12	3	—
Mehsana	21 (23.86)	—	—	12	5	4
Surendranagar	24 (27.27)			13	6	5
Total	88 100.00	— (NIL)	7 7.95	53 60.23	17 19.32	11 12.50

In the district of Mehsana, out of 21 households no one was using all the 3 inputs, 12 were using 2 inputs, 5 were using one input and 4 did not use any input. In the district of Surendranagar, there was no household out of 24 using 3 inputs. However, there were 13 households using 2 inputs, 6 using one input and 5 using no input. This shows that the district of Ahmedabad is more advanced in terms of using inputs for getting better harvest. It should also be noted that there was no household out of the total of 88 who were reported to have used multiple inputs for inprovement of agriculture. The overall position shows that there were 7.95 per cent of households using 3 inputs, 60.23 per cent using 2 inputs, 19.32 per cent using one input and 12.50 per cent of households using none.

In Table 6.15, we present the data indicating the number of households using chemical fertilizers, insecticides, hybrid seeds and new tools, etc. In all, there were 65 households using chemical fertilizers, 5 using insecticides, 72 using hybrid seeds and 2 using new tools or technology. This shows that the use of insecticides and new technology was extremely low among the scheduled castes landholders. This may be because of the small plots of land cultivated by them and also their inability to go in for costly innovations. With regard to the use of chemical

TABLE 6.15 Specific Types of Inputs Used by Households

District	No.of H.H.	Chemical Fertilisers No.of H.H.	Insecti-cides No.of H.H.	Hybride seeds No.of H.H.	New tools and devices H.H.
Ahmedabad	26 (29.55)	22	3	23	2
Kaira	17 (19.32)	17	2	14	—
Mehsana	21 (23.86)	12	—	17	—
Surendranagar	24 (27.27)	14	—	18	—
Total	88*	65	5	72	2

* Totals do not tally due to overlapping categories

fertilizers and hybrid seeds, Ahmedabad stood first in all the sample households of 4 districts. The district of Surendranagar was relatively better off in the use of chemical fertilizers and hybrid seeds as compared to Kaira and Mehsana. In Table 6.16, we present information on the use of each of the major inputs in combination with other inputs used by the scheduled castes farmers. There were in all 72 households of which 12 used hybrid seeds alone, 53 used hybrid seeds in combination with

TABLE 6.16 Hybrid Seeds Used in Combination with Other Inputs, etc.

District	No.of H.H.	Hybrid seeds alone	Hybrid seeds with fertilizers	Hybrid seeds with insecticides and fertilisers	Hybrid seeds with new tools and fertilisers
Ahmedabad	23	2	16	3	2
Kaira	14	—	12	2	—
Mehsana	17	5	12	—	—
Surendranagar	18	5	13	—	—
Total	72 (100.00)	12 (16.67)	53 (73.61)	5 (6.94)	2 (2.78)

fertilizers, 5 used gybrid seeds with insecticides and fertilizers and 2 used the same with new tools and fertilizers. The number of households using various combinations of inputs for improving agriculture was 23, the highest in Ahmedabad and this was followed by less number of 17 and 18 households in Mehsana and Surendranagar respectively. The district of Kaira had only 14 households using hybrid seeds alongwith other inputs. The major innovation in agriculture in relation to the traditional method of using organic manner was the increasing use of chemical fertilizers by the farmers. The data on the use of chemical fertilizers in combination with other inputs are presented in Table 6.17. In all, there were 65 households out of 88 landholders using chemical fertilizers. Those who used only chemical fertilizers and nothing else were 5 households. On the other hand, there were 53 households using fertilizers in combination with hybrid seeds and only 5 households were using fertilizers alongwith the hybrid seeds and insecticides. In the end, there were 2 households using all the other inputs along with the technology. The SC landholders in the districts of Ahmedabad and Kaira were relatively better placed in the use of chemical fertilizers. The use of the same in the districts of Surendranagar and Mehsana was relatively low.

The general information on households using insecticides in combination with other inputs is interesting. There were only 5 households using insecticides alongwith the fertilizers and hybrid seeds. There was no landholder using insecticides in Surendaranagar while in Ahmedabad, there were 3 households using that innovation.

In the same way, the use of new tools and technology was quite disappointing. There were only 2 households from Ahmedabad and none

TABLE 6.17 Chemical Fertilisers Used in Combination with Other Inputs

District	No. of H.H. using chemical fertilisers	Only ferti-lisers	Ferti-lisers and Hybrid seeds	Ferti-lisers with insecti-cides and Hybrid seeds	Ferti-lisers, etc. and new techno-logy
Ahmedabad	22 (33.86)	1	16	3	2
Kaira	17 (26.15)	3	12	2	—
Mehsana	12 (18.46)	—	12	—	—
Surendranagar	14 (21.54)	1	13	—	—
Total	65 (100.00)	5 (7.69)	53 (81.54)	5 (7.69)	2 (3.08)

from Kaira, Mehsana and Surendranagar using new technology for improvement of agriculture. These two households reported from Ahmedabad said that whenever they were hard-pressed with time, they took tractors on hire for cultivating their land. It also indicates that they did not have bullocks for ploughing nor other implements useful for undertaking appropriate tilling operations in the field.

Now we shall throw some additional light on the use of inputs and technology by the scheduled castes landholders. In Table 6.18, we find that out of 88 landholders, there were 72 using improved seeds, 65 chemical fertilizers, 5 insecticides and 2 using new technology. In terms of the area in hectare of land where various inputs were used, we find that improved seeds were used in 182.17 hectares of land by 72 households. In the same way, chemical fertilizers were used in 141.41 hectares by 65 households. So far as insecticides and new technology were concerned, we have crops in 3.29 hectares treated by chemical fertilizers by 5 households and there were only 2.20 hectares of land where the use of new technology, particularly occasional use of tractors was reported. It is clear that Ahmedabad landholders were most advanced in use of improved seeds, fertilizers, insecticides and new technology. The status of Surendranagar scheduled castes landholders was also relatively better than those of Kaira and Mehsana in this respect.

In Table 6.19, we have data on use of insecticides per hectare per annum. The total area under cultivation in all the 4 districts was 242.77

TABLE 6.18 Use of Inputs and New Technology in Agriculture

District	Gross crop area		Area covered under							
			Improved seeds		Chemical Fertilisers		Insecticides		New tools and technology	
	No.of H.H.	Area (Hect.)	No.of H.H.	Area (Hect.)	No.of H.H.	Area (Hect.)	No.of H.H.	Area (Hect.)	No.of H.H.	Area (Hect.)
Ahmedabad	26	66.62	23	46.30	22	51.36	3	1.26	2	2.20
Kaira	17	20.17	14	15.69	17	16.95	2	2.03	—	—
Mehsana	21	51.00	17	39.62	12	11.83	—	—	—	—
Surendranagar	24	104.98	18	80.56	14	61.27	—	—	—	—
Total	88 (100.00)	242.77 (100.00)	72 (81.82)	182.17 (74.90)	65 (73.86)	141.41 (58.02)	5 (5.68)	3.29 (0.04)	2 (2.27)	2.20 (0.03)

* *Totals do not tally due to overlapping categories.*

hectares of land of which only 3.29 hectares were treated with insecticides. The amount of insecticides used in this area was 10 litres and the average use per hectare came to be 7.04 litres. The total cost of the insecticides amounted to Rs. 190 and the cost per hectare came to be Rs. 58. It was interesting to note that no one used chemical fertilizers in the districts of Mehsana and Surendranagar. If we go by the amount of insecticides used, we find that SC landholders in Ahmedabad used 7 litres out of the total of 10 litres used by landhoders in 4 districts. The use of insecticides in the district of Kaira was reported to be 3.00 litres.

TABLE 6.19 Use of Insecticides Per Annum

District	Total area under cultivation (Hect.)	Area treated with insecticides (Hect)	Total measure of insecticide used in litres	Average use per Hectare in litres	Total cost of insecticide Rs.	Cost of insecticide Rs.
Ahmedabad	66.62	1.26	7.00	5.56	118	94
Kaira	20.17	2.03	3.00	1.48	72	36
Mehsana	51.00	—	—	—	—	—
Surendranagar	104.98	—	—	—	—	—
Total	242.77	3.29	10.00	7.04	190	58

In Table 6.20, we have data on the use of hybrid seeds per hectare per annum. The total area covered by use of hybrid seeds amounted to 182.17 hectares. The amount of hybrid seeds used amounted to 88.31

TABLE 6.20 Use of Hybrid Seeds Per Annum

District	Total area under cultivation (Hect.)	Area covered by hybrid seeds (Hect.)	Total amount of hybrid seeds used in quintal	Average use per hectare in quintal	Total cost of hybrid seeds used Rs.	Cost of hybrid seeds per Hectare Rs.
Ahmedabad	66.62 (27.44)	46.30	15.20 (17.21)	0.33	2458 (17.96)	53
Kaira	20.17 (8.31)	15.69	19.60 (22.19)	1.00	2065 (15.09)	132
Mehsana	51.00 (21.01)	39.62	16.31 (18.47)	0.41	3158 (23.08)	80
Surendranagar	104.98 (43.24)	80.56	37.20 (42.12)	0.46	6002 (43.86)	74
Total	242.77 (100.00)	182.17 (75.04)	88.31 (100.00)	0.48 (0.54)	13683 (100.00)	75 (0.55)

quintals. This means that the average use of seeds per hectare came to be 0.48 quintals only. In terms of cost of hybrid seeds, we find that Rs.13,683 were spent by the landholders in all the 4 districts. The cost of hybrid seeds per hectare came to be Rs.75 only. The average cost of hybrid seeds per hectare in the districts of Kaira was the highest and it came to be Rs. 132. In the district of Mehsana and Surendranagar also, the landholders were spending relatively more money than in the district of Ahmedabad. The district of Kaira was way ahead of almost all the districts in use of hybrid seeds, specially when the total area cultivated by scheduled castes landholders was only 20.17 hectares.

The Table 6.21 throws light on the use of chemical fertilisers per hectare per annum. The total area treated by chemical fertilisers was 141.41 hectares and the amount of fertilisers used comes to be 147.60 quintals. This means that on an average, the scheduled castes landholders used 2.68 quintals of chemical fertilizers per hectare. The total cost of chemical fertilizers used in all the 4 districts was Rs. 36,025 and the cost per hectare came to be Rs. 255. It is interesting to note that in all the 3 districts, such as Ahmedabad, Kaira and Surendranagar, the cost of fertilizers used per hectare was much lower than the average cost incurred in Mehsana. This unique result appeared because of the fact that in the district of Mehsana, the total area treated by 32.50 quintals of fertilizers was only 11.83 hectares. It seems that the scheduled castes households used irrigation as a means to take multiple crops in small area.

TABLE 6.21 Use of Chemical Fertilisers Per Hectare Per Annum

District	Total area under cultivation (Hect.)	Area treated by chemical fertilisers (Hect.)	Total amount of chemical fertiliser in quintal	Average use per hectare in quintal	Total cost of fertiliser used Rs	Cost of fertilizer per hectare Rs
Ahmedabad	66.62 (27.44)	51.36	44.00 (29.81)	0.86	10747 (29.83)	209
Kaira	20.17 (8.31)	16.95	20.60 (13.96)	1.00	5026 (13.95)	297
Mehsana	51.00 (21.01)	11.83	32.50 (22.02)	3.00	7930 (22.01)	670
Surendranagar	104.98 (43.24)	61.27	50.50 (34.21)	0.82	12322 (34.20)	201
Total	242.77 (100.00)	141.41 (58.25)	147.60 (100.00)	2.68 (1.82)	36025 (100.00)	255 (0.71)

The cost of fertiliser per hectare in Surendranagar was the lowest *i.e.*

Rs. 201, possibly because 61.27 hectares were treated by fertilisers out of 104.98 hectares of land which was the highest amount of land in all the 4 districts.

Income, Expenditure, Sale and Consumption

In this section, we shall throw light on net income, expenditure, sale, etc., of households from agriculture, income in combination with other occupations and the same for different categories of farmers.

In Table 6.22, we present a classification of gross annual income from agricultural produce, expenditure, net income, consumption, etc. It has been indicated earlier that out of 105, the number of households who were able to earn income from agriculture were 88. The income from total agricultural produce of all these households was Rs. 4,10,775. The income per household in all the 4 districts came to be Rs. 4,668. The total expenditure incurred by all the households on agriculture was Rs. 1,71,308 and the expenditure per household came to be Rs. 1,947. This means that the net income from agriculture for all the households was Rs. 2,39,467 and the same per household came to be Rs. 2,721.

It is interesting to note that the domestic consumption of agricultural produce for all the households was worth Rs. 66,340. This shows that every household consumed agricultural produces not more than worth Rs. 754 only. In contrast to the domestic consumption of agricultural produce, we find that the sale was much higher. The total produce sold by all the households was worth Rs. 1,37,127. This means that every household sold the agricultural produce worth Rs. 1,967 per year.

When we look at district wise position regarding the surplus income from agricultural produce of scheduled castes landholders, we find that Ahmedabad was in deficit (of produce) worth Rs. 52 per annum. On the other hand, the district of Surendranagar had a surplus worth Rs. 2,138 per household. Mehsana was the next in the category of having surplus worth Rs. 1,613 and last came the district of Kaira with surplus worth Rs. 1,349.

In Table 6.23, we present a classification of agricultural income by sub-castes of scheduled castes. It is significant to note that there were 54 households of Vankar sub-caste getting the total income of Rs. 1,47,123 from agriculture. Next in the rank came the sub-caste of Chamar numbering 25 households and earning agricultural income worth Rs. 80,488. The agricultural income of the sub-castes of Valmiki and Senva was around Rs. 1,000. However, it is clear that 2 Senva households were better placed in income from agriculture than 7 Valmiki households.

TABLE 6.22 Gross Annual Income, Expenditure, Net Income, etc. from Agricultural Produce

District	No.of H.H. with income from land	Total income from agricultural produce		Total expenditure on agriculture		Net income from agriculture		Domestic consumption of produce.		Income of sale of produce	
		Income in Rs.	Income per H.H. Rs.	Expenditure in Rs.	Expenditure Per H.H. in Rs.	Income in Rs. Net	Income per H.H. in Rs. Net	Consumption in Rs.	Consumption per H.H. in Rs.	Income in Rs.	Income per H.H. in Rs.	Surplus per H.H. worth Rs.
Ahmedabad	26	93798	3608	43433	1670	50365	1938	25857	995	24508	943	-52.00
Kaira	17	61648	3626	15119	889	46529	2737	11803	694	34726	2043	+1349.00
Mehsana	21	108459	5165	42298	2015	66161	3151	16130	769	50031	2382	+1613.00
Surendranagar	24	146870	6120	70458	2935	76412	3184	12550	523	63862	2661	+2138.00
Total	88	410775	4668	171308	1947	239467	2721	66340	754	173127	1967	+1213.00

TABLE 6.23 Agricultural Income of the SC Sub-castes

District	Names of sub-castes Households											
			Vankar		Chamar		Valmiki		Garoda		Senva	
	No.of H.H.	Income in Rs.	No.of H.H.	Income in Rs.	No.of H.H.	Income in Rs.	No.of H.H.	Income in Rs.	No.of H.H.	Income in Rs.	No. of H.H.	Income in Rs.
Ahmedabad	26	50365	17	35231	8	14239	—	—	—	—	1	895
Kaira	17	46529	9	21187	4	18943	4	6399	—	—	—	—
Mehsana	21	66161	11	25636	8	39060	1	875	—	—	1	590
Surendranagar	24	76412	17	65069	5	8246	2	3097	—	—	—	—
Total	88 (100.00)	239467 (100.00)	54 (61.36)	147123 (61.44)	25 (28.41)	80488 (33.61)	7 (7.95)	10371 (4.33)	— —	— —	2 (2.27)	1485 (0.62)

There was no Garoda households with income from agricultural land.

We shall now throw light on annual agricultural income of sample households in combination with other occupations in general. The data presented in Table 6.24 throws light on whether the households received income from agriculture as only principal or as subsidiary occupation. There were only 8 households who were dependent entirely on agriculture. Their total income came to be Rs. 40,495 and the income per household came to be Rs. 5062. Those households who had taken agriculture as principal occupation and were earning money by other means also, were 27. Their total income per annum was Rs. 1,26,394 and income per household came to be Rs. 4,682. These groups of households had almost equal income as compared to those who were engaged in agriculture alone. The remaining 53 out of 88 housheholds were earning their income from agriculture as a subsidiary occupation. Their economic position was very much below the income of those who practiced agriculture alone or as principal occupation.

In Table 6.25, we present a consolidated annual income of households having agriculture as only or principal occupation. The total number of such households was 35 and their consolidated income was Rs. 2,27,737. This means that the average income per household came to be Rs. 6,507. In contrast to this, their average income from other occupations came to be Rs. 1,738 and that from agriculture came to be Rs. 4,768.

In Table 6.26, we are presenting the data on income from agriculture according to the category oflandholder. There were 27 marginal landholders with the annual income of Rs. 46,576 from agriculture. The income of marginal farmer per household came to be Rs. 1,968 only. The income of the smaller farmers, who number 35, was in all Rs. 76,357 and their average income came to be Rs. 2,182, which was slightly higher than the average income of the marginal farmer per hosehold. The number of medium farmers was 19 having Rs. 69,611 as total income from agriculture. The income per household of these categories of farmers was Rs. 3,664. In the end, there were 7 big farmers with the total income of Rs. 46,923 and per HH Rs. 17,795. This means that the income of big farmers per household was nearly five times the income per household of medium farmers. The trend of descending order from there on is passed on to small farmers and marginal farmers who were placed at the lowest level in the income of agriculture per household.

In Table 6.27, we present the data on income and area of land for all the 105 land owning households whether they were practising agriculture alone, as principal or alongwith other occupations. There were 8 households who were entirely dependent on agriculture alone and had the income of

TABLE 6.24 Income from Agriculture as Principal or Subsidiary Occupation

District	Income from agriculture alone			Income from agriculture as principal occupation			Income from agriculture as subsidiary occupation			Total income from agriculture		
	No. of H.H.	Rs. Total	Rs. Per H.H.	No. of H.H.	Rs. Total	Rs. Per H.H.	No. of H.H.	Rs. total	Rs. Per H.H.	No. of H.H.	Rs. Total	Rs. Per H.H.
Ahmedabad	2	7450	3725	6	20473	3413	18	22442	1247	26	50365	1938
Kaira	4	24293	6073	2	3375	1688	11	18861	1715	17	46529	2737
Mehsana	—	—	—	7	45570	6510	14	20591	1471	21	66161	3151
Surendranagar	2	8752	4356	12	56976	4748	10	10684	1069	24	76421	3184
Total	8 (9.09)	40495 (16.91)	5062	27 (30.68)	126394 (52.78)	4682	53 (60.23)	72578 (30.31)	1369	88 (100.00)	239467 (100.00)	2722

TABLE 6.25 Annual Income of Households with Agriculture as Principal Occupation (in Rs.)

District	No. of H.H.	Consolidated Income	Consolidated average per Household	Income from agriculture as principal occupation	Average per H.H. from agriculture	Income from other occupations	Average per H.H. from other occupations.
Ahmedabad	8	43421	5428	27930	3490	15498	1937
Kaira	6	29288	4882	27668	4611	1628	270
Mehasana	7	66370	9482	45570	6510	20800	2971
Surendrangar	14	88658	6333	65728	3545	22930	1637
Total	35	227737	6507	166889	4768	60848	1738

TABLE 6.26 Income of Household by Size of Landholdings

District	Marginal farmer			Small farmer			Medium farmer			Big farmer			Total		
	No. of H.H.	Total Income	Income per H.H.	No. of H.H.	Total Income	Income per H.H.	No. of H.H.	Total Income	Income per H.H.	No. of H.H.	Total Income	Income per H.H.	No. of H.H.	Total Income	Income per H.H.
Ahmedabad	7	9453	1350	15	21558	1437	3	7585	2462	1	11969	11969	26	50365	1937
Kaira	10	10088	1909	5	16391	3278	2	11050	5525	—	—	—	17	46529	2737
Mehsana	7	13875	1982	10	28286	2829	4	24000	6000	—	—	—	21	66161	3151
Surendranagar	3	4160	1387	5	10122	2024	10	27176	2718	6	34954	5826	24	76412	3184
Total	27	46576	1986	35	76357	2182	19	69611	3664	7	46923	17795	88	239467	2721

Rs. 194.99 per hectare. There were 27 households principally dependent on agriculture with a total income of Rs. 1,26,394 with the income of Rs. 4,847 per hectare. The next group of households dependent on occupations other than agriculture were 53. The total income of these households from agriculture was Rs. 72,578 and their income per hectare came to be only Rs. 11.77. In the end,there were 17 households who had no income from agriculture, even though they had a total of 41.68 hectares of land.

TABLE 6.27 Households Earning Income from Agriculture Alone or in Combination with Other Occupations

Categories of Households by occupation	No. of H.H. owning land	Income from agricul-ture	Size of land in Hect.	Income per H.H.	Income per Hectare
H.H. dependent on agriculture alone	8	40495	25.96	5062	194.99
H.H. dependent on agriculture as principal occupation	27	126394	96.58	4681	48.47
H.H. dependent on other occupations as main	53	72578	116.03	1369	11.77
H.H. having no income from land	17	—	41.68	—	—
Total	105	239467	280.25	2281	8.14

7

LAND MORTGAGE AND RELATED ISSUES

Introduction

The problem of land mortgage has been perennial problem for the marginal and small farmers in particular in rural areas. Before Independence, this problem was felt more acutely because of lack of government protection to some of those farmers who had to work as agricultural labourers. They needed money on account of various unforseen events in life such as sickness, accident, untimely death, etc. Money was needed also on happy social occasions to be celebrated by the family. The crust of custom was so heavily weighed on almost all categories of rural peasantry that they could not escape easily from such expenditure to upkeep their prestige in the society.

Even the poorest household was sometimes compelled by caste leaders to spent money on offering feasts to the castemen at the time of death, marriage, etc. Added to this pressure, the poorer village people suffered due to large families and uncertain annual income on account of draught or pestilence. Above all, the rise in the cost of living remained unbearable.

The scheduled castes, who form largest proportion of agricultural labourers in our country, were the worst hit victims of the customary burden for which they had to incur heavy debts. Sometimes, the son in a poor scheduled castes family instead of inheriting a tangible property to standby, inherited debts either from father or forefathers. The most valued asset in rural areas has always been a piece of agricultural land, and a person who was in debt had no alternative but to mortagage full or part of the land possessed by him to moneylender. There have been many patterns of mortagaging land by a poor farmer to a money-lender who may be a rich landholder or a businessman in rural areas. When a person was in need of money, he was not given the full amount he required at a point of time. The borrowed money often came to him initially on the basis of the word of mouth and without written agreements whatsoever. The interest at which the money was advanced as loan was generally with compound interest, and when the loan was repaid in different instalments over a period of time, the rate of interest and the amount to be paid to the money lender became usurious. Often a person in debt was not able to pay the interest on the loan taken by him, he was thus pressurised by the moneylender to sell his land to him. The produce of the land he cultivated was every year adjusted with the total interest which had to be paid to the moneylender. Sometimes the income of crops from the land was more than sufficient to cover up the interest that had to be paid by the land-holder. However, the assessment of the income from land was made at the whim and fancy of the moneylender or the rich landlord in such a manner that year after year there was no decrease in the basic amount taken on loan by the poor debtor. When the original debt remained unpaid under the usurious practice of the moneylender as indicated above, for a few years, the landholder was compelled to sign a mortgage deed. Quite a few scheduled castes landholders surveyed during this study were the victims of this kind of cruel practice perpetrated by the money-lenders.

It will be interesting to make some general observations on the commitment involved in signing of a mortagage deed by a poor farmer under the circumstances of moral pressure and economic obligations. The poor in general is so god fearing that their commitment to moral obligation sometimes became greater burden than other kinds of obligations. Social obligations were also treated as a part of moral obligation and they continued to remain in a vicious circle of discharging their obligations by incurring, sometimes frequently, beyond their means. We shall now throw some light on general conditions under which the mortgagie deed vis-a-vis land for cultivation is executed.

Land Mortgage to Private Moneylenders

As it is well known, the whole business of mortgage of land is a highly shady business. Therefore, the mechanisms employed by a landlord or a moneylender are generally full of intrigues and deceit. The ultimate aim of the moneylender is to liquidate the land of a poor farmer for good. The illegal and outrageous means employed in the transactions of land mortgage by interested parties are summarised in the following points :

(i) If a person taking loan is extremely poor and needy, he is compelled to surrender his land to be used by the moneylender simply on oral agreement;

(ii) The terms of agreement of mortgage, whether oral or on a piece of paper, are extremely tight, in the sense that even grass growing on the mortgaged land becomes the property of the moneylender;

(iii) The agreements written on plain paper with full or partial value of court stamp required for legal transaction or written on court stamp paper of smaller denomination issued by the government. Both these categories of mortgage deeds are invalid in a court of law;

(iv) In addition to the the above means of cheating a mortgager of land, more criminal and heinous practices are adopted in which the signature or the thumb impression on the mortgage deed is altered. Besides, a dummy signature can always be used for executing final liquidation of the land of the original mortgager, through a court of law; and

(v) During the whole period of mortgage deed, it is the original landholder who has to pay the land revenue to the government, without any liability imposed on the moneylender.

It is significant to note that when the Prime Minister's 20 Point Programme was implemented, there was a provision of using Debt Redemption Act which amounted to abolition of the debts to be paid by the farmers claiming free hold of his land previously held by him. With this new legal position of land mortgage deed, under the Presidential Order of Debt Redemption Act effected sometimes in 1978, both the moneylender and the landlords were put into difficulty. This unusually radical situation led to convenient interpretation by different parties of the Presidential Order regarding land mortgage deeds.

A landholder, whose land was mortgaged, thought that he had a right to take the possession of his land and reap whatever harvest desired by him. He tried to physically capture the land, but was prevented by the landlords to whom land was mortgaged. This called for interference by the law and order officers *i.e.* policemen whose help was sought by the landlords. The police accepted the bonafide possession of the land by the moneylender on the basis of the stamped paper of mortgage deed shown to them. The land owners, who were prevented from taking possession of their land on the basis of the Presidential Order, went to the court of law in order to see that the land was restored to them as bonafide landholders. The court could not move immediately in favour of the poor landholders because the police were made to act in favour of the moneylender who had obtained the government certificate of being in possession of land on the strength of mortgage deed signed by the landholder.

It was not possible to deal with the legal aspects of this subject full of complications on account of different circumstances attached to each case of mortgage in sub-divisional courts of Ahmedabad District. The terms and conditions of the deeds vary a great deal from case to case. However, one expected in vain the element of uniformity in the treatment of all the cases under legal provisions. It will be useful to cite an outstanding instant of the judgement in the Narol Court on a suit filed by a few landholders against moneylenders or landlords who were not prepared to restore possession of their land on the basis of the Presidential Order promulgating the Debt Redemption Act.

In the first instance, the Narol Court gave the judgment in favour of landlords but the poor landowners filed a writ petition urging the High Court to see that their land was evacuated by the moneylenders and given entry and possession and self-cultivation. In the end, when the court gave hearing on the petition filed by the poor landowners, it was declared that the old land mortgage deeds in favour of the moneylenders tentamount to the breach of the conditions of the Presidential Order and therefore, all the previous deeds empowering the moneylender to enjoy the land of the poor landholders are considered null and void. It may be noted that the concerned 3 scheduled castes households had lost the case in Dholka Court but won in Narol Court. One of the important clauses of this judgement was that since the moneylenders were not registered, they had no right to hold up the land of the poor SC landholders who borrowed mony from them.

Resolving Cases of Land Mortgage

It may be noted that inspite of the Debt Redemption Act 1978 being in operation, there were cases of underhand dealings of moneylenders trying to usurp the land of the indebted poor landholders. The institution called Bharatiya Khet-Majur Sangh, Gujarat, had become active in certian areas of Gujarat in order to fight cases in a court of law on behalf of the landholders. The case fought at the Narol Court referred to earlier was taken care of by the above voluntary organisation.

It will be useful to record here what Shantaben Makwana, President, Akhil Bharat Anusuchit Jati Parishad, Gujarat Branch, observed on the subject in a thought-provoking article published in 1983.* "Mortgage

* Shantaben Makwana, "From Lending money to grabbing land", *Parishad Sandesh*, Vol. 1, No. 5, 1983, pp.18-19.

deeds obtained under duress or by fraud or misrepresentation deserve to be treated as invalid. The so called mortgage deeds whereby scheduled castes have been deprived of their agricultural lands can be proved to be invalid for the reasons noted below":

1. There are veiled money-lending transactions under cover of manifest mortgage transaction, the *Zamindar* or *Sahukar* does not hold a licence under the Money-Lenders Act.
2. The scheduled caste cultivator is shown in the government records as holder of mortagaged land, generally paying the revenue and other dues in respect of the land.
3. According to the Transfer of Property Act, and the Indian Registration Act, registration of mortgage deeds is compulsory, but in practice the money lending *Zamindars* or *Sahukars* evades registration.
4. According to the terms of the land grant to landholder, the lands are virtually inalienable, hence the mortage transation amounts to the breach of conditions of grant.

The Cases of Land Mortagage

In this section, we shall present the data of present sample survey throwing light on various aspects of the land mortgage deeds and socio-economic status of the households of scheduled castes concerned. Eventhough the total of 13 cases of land mortagage out of 105 landholders were not many, we have interesting findings which reveal the extent to which the problem of land mortgage was faced by households of the scheduled castes covered by this study.

In Table 7.1, we find that there were only 13 households who

TABLE 7.1 Households Who Mortgaged Agricultural Land

District	Total sample H.H. and land		Cases of mortgage		Percentage of total	
	No. of H.H.	Area in Hect.	No. of H.H.	Area in Hect.	No. of H.H.	Area in Hect.
Ahmedabad	30	65.56	6	7.71	20.00	0.14
Kaira	18	18.55	—	—	—	—
Mehsana	25	49.86	6	5.22	24.00	0.10
Surendranagar	32	146.28	1	6.40	3.13	0.04
Total	105	280.25	13	19.33	12.38	0.07

mortgaged land to money lender. The total area of land mortgaged by these households was 19.33 hectares out of the total of 280.25 hectares owned by 105 households. This means that 12.38 per cent of the households mortgaged, on an average 0.07 per cent of land. It seems that not much damage was done to the scheduled castes households who mortgaged their land. But this is only a superflous impression because in reality, the land that was mortgaged was most fertile and therefore, the very act of losing smallest area of rich land becomes disastrous to the status of a scheduled caste family.

The duration for which land was mortgaged by 13 households indicated above is presented in Table 7.2. The table reveals that 5 households mortgaged 8.90 hectares of land for borrowing a total amount of Rs. 21,500 for a period of 1 to 2 years. Besides, there were other 3 households who mortgaged total of 3.33 hectares of land against Rs. 11,400 for a period of 3 to 4 years. There were two households who mortgaged 2.00 hectares of land against Rs. 15,000 for a period of 7 to 8 years. Those who mortgaged land for more than 9 to 30 years period were only 3 households. In this group, one case was outstanding because the area of land mortgaged by that particular household was 3.20 hectares as against the borrowing of Rs. 750 only. The overall picture that emerges is that 13 households mortgaged land for borrowing Rs. 55,150 against 19.33 hectares of land.

TABLE 7.2 Size of Land Mortgaged by Time and Loan Taken

Approximate period of mortgage before 1983	No. of H.H.	Mortgaged area in Hect.	Amount of loan or debt Rs.
1 to 2 years	5	8.90	21,500
3 to 4 years	3	3.33	11,400
7 to 8 years	2	2.00	15,000
9 to 10 years	1	1.20	500
11 to 12 years	—	—	—
12 to 13 years	—	—	—
13 to 15 years	1	0.69	6,500
16 to 30 years	1	3.20	750
Total	13	19.33	55,150

In Table 7.3, we have presented classification of cases of partial or entire land mortgage by scheduled castes households concerned. The overall picture shows that there were 8 households who mortgaged all the land in their possession making a total area of 14.64 hectares of land. There were 5 households on the other hand who mortgaged only 4.69 hectares of land while remaining areas were kept for self cultivation. It seems reasonable to presume that the partial pløts of land mortgaged by 5 households were of best quality as insisted usually by the money lender. One can imagine the great set-back to the income of the households concerned.

TABLE 7.3 Cases of Partial and Complete Land Mortgaged

District	No. of H.H.	Area in Hect.	Types of cases of mortgage of land			
			Entire land		Partial land	
			No. of H.H.	Area in Hect.	No. of H.H.	Area in Hect.
Ahmedabad	6	7.71	3	4.69	3	3.02
Kaira	—	—	—	—	—	—
Mehsana	6	5.22	4	3.55	2	1.67
Surendranagar	1	6.40	1	6.40	—	—
Total	13	19.33	8	14.64	5	4.69

We shall now throw light on different categories of landholders who were compelled to mortgage land for borrowing money in times of stress and strain. The data on this subject are presented in Table 7.4. There were 4 cases of households belonging to marginal landholders who mortgaged 2.69 hectares of land which was their entire agricultural holdings. It is significant to note that the marginal landholders among scheduled castes have so small plots that the problem of partial mortgage of land just does not arise. In contrast to this, there was no big landholder among the

TABLE 7.4 Land Mortgaged by Categories of Landhoders

Category of landholders	Cases of total land mortgage		Cases of partial land mortgage		Total	
	No. of H.H.	Area in Hect.	No. of H.H.	Area in Hect.	No. of H.H.	Area in Hect.
Marginal	4	2.69	—	—	4	2.69
Small	2	2.35	2	1.24	4	3.59
Medium	2	9.60	3	3.45	5	13.05
Big	—	—	—	—	—	—
Total	8	14.64	5	4.69	13	19.33

scheduled castes who mortgaged land. Among the small and medium size landholders, we have 2 households each who mortgaged their total land to the tune of 2.39 and 9.60 hectares respectively. Those who mortgaged a part of their land, the number of small and medium size landholders were 2 and 3 respectively.

In Table 7.5, we have classification of households giving land on mortgage not to outside moneylender but to members of various castes in the village. The data throws light on the amount of loan received by the concerned scheduled castes households from the members of various castes. The overall picture shows that the total amount of loan advanced by 7 castes or community and sub-castes to the households of scheduled castes was Rs. 55,150. This means that the average loan taken per household came to be Rs. 4,242. The most outstanding case is of a Patel moneylender who had given a total loan of Rs. 17,000 to three SC households. It is interesting to note that there was one scheduled caste household who received a loan of Rs. 12,000 from a Muslim money-lender. The other significant case was of a Kumbhar moneylender who advanced a loan of Rs. 6,000 to one scheduled castes household. The other category of petty money lenders come from the caste of *Darbar* (Rajput), *Thakore*, *Vanand* (Barbar) and *Suthar* (Carpenter).

TABLE 7.5 Land Mortgaged to Members of Various Castes

Sub-castes	No. of H.H.	Area in Hect.	Total amount of loan Rs.	Loan per H.H. Rs.
Darbar	3	5.09	7250	2416
Thakore	3	2.82	6900	2300
Patel	3	7.24	17000	5666
Muslim	1	1.20	12000	12000
Vanand	1	0.80	3000	3000
Kumbhar	1	1.38	6000	6000
Suthar	1	0.80	3000	3000
Total	13	19.33	55150	4242

In Table 7.6, we have data throwing light on the purpose for which money was borrowed by scheduled castes households. There were 5 households who borrowed Rs. 24,500 as against 4.07 hectares of land for the purpose of meeting expenditures on social occasions. In the next category, 2 households borrowed money during sickness in the family for which they mortgaged 1.24 hectares of land against Rs. 11,000. There were 5 households, possibily from those below poverty line, who had mortgaged 12.64 hectares of land for borrowing Rs. 13,650 in order to take care of their subsistence during the period of want. It is significant to note that there was only one household who felt the necessity of mortgaging 1.38 hectares of land for borrowing Rs. 6,000 in order to repair the irrigation well in the field.

TABLE 7.6 The Purpose of Mortgaging Land

Purpose	No.of H.H.	Area in Hect.	Total Amt. of Loan Rs.	Loan per H.H. Rs.
On social occasion	5	4.07	24500	4900
During sickness in family	2	1.24	11000	5500
For subsistance during period of want	5	12.64	13650	2730
For making or repairing fieldwell	1	1.38	6000	6000
Total	13	19.33	55150	4242

The data presented in Table 7.7 throws light on the mechanism under which a scheduled caste landholder was compelled to mortgage his land to the moneylender. Generally, the moneylender indulges in underhand practices while preparing the deeds for advancing money. It is revealed from the study of the 13 scheduled castes households that in one case the moneylender got a mortgage deed signed on stamped paper of Rs. 5.50 only against a loan of Rs. 3,000. The area of land mortgaged in this particular case was 0.80 hectares only. There are 5 cases of house-holds

TABLE 7.7 Methods of Mortgaging Land

Open or concealed practices of mortgage	No.of H.H.	Mortgaged area in Hect.	Amount of loan or debt Rs.
On court stamp paper of Rs. 5.50	1	0.80	3,000
On court stamp paper of Rs. 5.00	5	4.11	26,000
On paper with 20 paise Revenue Stamp	2	1.55	8,400
On plain paper agreement	5	12.87	17,750
Total	13	19.33	55,150

who borrowed in all Rs. 26,000 against 4.11 hectares of land mortgaged to moneylenders on the stamp paper worth Rs. 5 only. There were two cases where only 10 or 20 paise revenue stamp was used for signing the mortgage deed involving Rs. 8,400 against 1.55 hectares of land. It is significant to note that there were 5 households of scheduled castes who mortgaged in all 12.87 hectares of land for borrowing Rs. 17,750, simply on plain paper.

We shall now figure out the extent to which the scheduled castes landholders, who mortgaged land to the moneylender, had to suffer from loss of income from the land given to the moneylender. This data is

TABLE 7.8 Loss of Income Due to Land Mortgaged to Moneylender

District	No. of H.H.	Mortgaged area in Hect.	Total income lost from land Rs.	Average income lost per Hect. Rs.	Average income lost per household Rs.
Ahmedabad	6	7.71	10856	1408	1809
Kaira	—	—	—	—	—
Mehsana	6	5.22	11103	2127	1850
Surendranagar	1	6.40	8953	1399	8953
Total	13	19.33	32706	1692	2516

presented district wise in Table 7.8. The table shows that there were 12 households with loss of average income per household amounting to Rs. 1,800 and more in the districts of Ahmedabad and Mehsana. This figure of loss of income per household in the district of Surendranagar was nearly eight times higher *i.e.* Rs. 8,953. In the district of Kaira, there was no household who had given land on mortgage, and therefore one can say that the evil of land mortgage among scheduled castes there was almost rare if not nil.

8

LAND FOR HOUSING

Introduction

One of the most acute problems faced by the masses of people in the 3rd World is to have adequate living conditions. In recent times, the World Health Organisation expressed great concern over the problem of housing in the countries of Asia and Africa. In India, the trend of population explosion is very serious. We shall have to provide for housing and schooling facilities for the fast rising young generation. The problem of housing is felt acute both in rural and urban areas. The problem of housing is, of course, the concern of the individuals. In view of the goal of socialistic pattern of the society, both the cooperative sector and the public sector will have to share responsibilities for taking care of housing not only for the middle classes, but also for the people living below poverty line. The problem of housing in the advanced countries in America and Europe is relatively easy to solve because there are housing agencies prepared to provide readymade houses on payment of instalments cut from salary of a person. There is no facility of this nature in our country because of various historical conditions of underdevelopment.

When we look at the problem of housing of the poor in rural areas, we confront innumerable problems. However, basic problem faced by scheduled castes and backward classes is of inability to have a house site for building ones own house. Most of the upper caste households in the villages of India are able to have a house of small or big size through inheritance or purchase. Most of the houses of upper castes are located in the plots determined by custom within the boundary of the village site. In certain parts of India, there have been provision of special small portions in one side of the village site where housing facilities are provided to scheduled castes and backward classes. Such facilities whether within the boundary of the village site or outside, such as SC Cheris in the South Indian village are inhabited mostly by the landless labourers. In view of rising trend in population of these people, there is acute shortage of living facilities for them. Sometimes the agricultural labourers are provided temporary sites for building their huts either in the common land of the village or in the land of the master for whom they work as landless labourers. But they constantly face the problem of evacuation if any dispute arises with regard to payment of wages for the agricultural labour in the fields. Since they live hand to mouth on almost all the days of the year, they have no capacity to buy a small piece of land for building their own houses.

Resolution to Provide Free House Sites

Looking to the fact that a large section of 70.00 per cent of agricultural labourers in rural areas are facing the difficulties of adequate living conditions, the government at the centre and in the states have come forward with a scheme to provide at least a small house site to begin with to agricultural labourers. The person, who is able to get a house site free of cost from the land under the jurisdiction of a village panchayat or from government waste land, has to spend his own money for building the house.

The Government of India, therefore, passed a resolution on 15-3-1972 directing the State Governments and the Union Territories to implement the programme of giving free of cost house sites to the poor persons in the rural areas. This directive of the Union Government was discussed by the Panchayat Parishads of the States in May 1972. The concerned officers in the States were informed on 11th May 1972 to implement the programme on the basis of following instructions regarding the acquisition of land, and prescribed time of putting this programme into action. The programme accordingly must be implemented:

(i) Within 15 days, if vacant plots of land are available in a village;
(ii) Within one month, if it is necessary to extend the boundary of village site by acquiring government or panchayat land or the land of the forest department; and
(iii) Within six months time, if it is necessary to acquire private land in the village.

Necessary instructions were issued to the officers concerned to allocate house sites free of cost to bonafide households. The decision to select households for presentation of free house sites had to be taken on the basis of criteria of eligibility prescribed in the following points:

(i) Households who do not own agricultural land or do not have a house or house site in the village;
(ii) Households whose main source of livelihood is agricultural labour; and
(iii) Households who are living during large part of the year in rural areas.

The above specific criteria of eligibility for receiving free house sites were made applicableto SCs and also to the households of artisans such as blacksmiths, carpenters, masons, shoe makers, tailors, potters, etc.

Method of Allocation of House Sites

The households who become eligible for getting free house sites are given a plot of 100 sq. yards for building the house. In order to improve the land to build a house, it was decided to give economic assistance within the range of Rs. 150 per household. The whole programme had to be implemented in a stipulated period of time and it was decided, therefore, to collect necessary information to facilitate the programme. The village officers concerned with implementing the programme had to make following advance preparations.

(a) To collect information regarding government waste land in every village;
(b) To make an estimated list of households of agricultural labourers, etc., in need of house sites;
(c) To help the households of agricultural labourers, etc., to make applications for getting house sites free of cost;
(d) To have the recommendations made for allocation of sites by the village Talati cum Mantri or Sarpanch of Village Panchayat; and
(e) To send the recommended applications for allocation of sites by the Land Committee at Taluka or District level. Arrangements had to be made for holding the meeting of Land Committee on the priority basis for allocation of house sites.

In view of the fact that the households of backward classes in general are hard pressed for adequate living facilities, it was decided to give priorities to them on the basis of the applications for house sites received by the authorities concerned. However, there were 4 specific conditions laid down for drawing up the list of households for allotment on the basis of priority.

(i) The 1st priority be given to landless agricultural labourers, who belong to scheduled castes, scheduled tribes and other backward classes;
(ii) Out of the above groups of people the first priority should be given to those households who have no house to live in;
(iii) Priority should be given to married persons above 18 years of age who have established separate hearths; and
(iv) After having covered the above categories of households for allotment of house sites on priority basis, the families of other groups of people who are landless agricultural labourers may be considered for allotment of house sites.

Conditions for Allotment of House Sites

The terms and conditions under which households are given free of cost house sites on priority basis in the rural areas are laid down in the following points:

(i) They will neither be permitted to exchange house sites allotted to them with others, nor allowed to divide them in smaller portions without the permission of the District Development Officer;
(ii) They will have to built the houses on the house sites within 2 years of the date of allotment of the plots;
(iii) They will have to pay the tax on the allotted non-agricultural land sites from the year of allotment;
(iv) They will not be permitted to give on rent the plots of the house sites nor any portion of the area built upon the same; and
(v) They will have to make personal efforts in order to get loan or subsidy for building the houses.

Process of Allotment of House Sites

To begin with, the Talati-cum-Mantri acquaints of details of the scheme to the members of target group eligible for allotment of house sites. After collection of applications of the households, they are forwarded to the Land Committee at the Taluka Level. The members of the Land Committee subsequently visit the villages concerned in a group or severally in order to scrutinise the applications collected by the Talati-cum-Mantri. At the time of scrutiny, the members of the Land Committee would process the information of the applicants in the presence of Sarpanch of the Village Panchayat, Chairman of Service Co-operative Society and traditional leaders of the village. Special care is to be taken in the cases where the applications of households were rejected by the Land Committee. In order to see that the rejection of applications of households is not made on arbitrary basis, the process of legal action is adopted. For this purpose, the custom of *Panchnama* is put into action and the decision of rejecting the application of a particular household is systematically argued out. It was found that when the members of the Land Committee paid collective visits to more than one village, at a time, it was difficult to scrutinise the eligibility of households for house-sites. There were many cases of injustice meted out to eligible households under these circumstances. It it was found that a particular village did not have enough land to be spared for allotment of free house sites to agricultural labourers, action was taken to get a resolution passed in the Panchayat of the village for further consideration of the cases to the District Collector in order to make the waste land or the pasture land availabe for house sites. Under such circumstances, the Circle Inspector or the Surveyor of the area would complete the process of allotment of house sites after the orders to this effect received from the District Collector.

It was reported that under this scheme, a total number of 4,07.135 households of the agricultural labourers were allotted house sites in Gujarat until 31st March 1980. Each plot of house sites measured 100 yards according to the basic plan of the scheme. Out of the total allotment of the house sites during this period, 87,600 house sites were allotted to the members of the scheduled castes. This means that 21.51 per cent of the total allotted plots were given to the scheduled castes households. It may be mentioned that the number of plots allotted to the households of scheduled tribes in Gujarat were 93,020 which comes to be 22.85 per cent of the total house sites allotted until the end of March 1980. It is interesting to note that the percentage of scheduled castes in the total population of the State of Gujarat is 7.00 per cent while that of the scheduled tribes is 14.00 per cent. This apparently shows that relatively the households of the scheduled castes have benefited more under the scheme than the households of the scheduled tribes. This is because a large number of scheduled castes households are settled in the planes where agriculture is practised than in hilly or forest area where tribals live. In any case, it is significant to note that taken together, these two groups of people received 44.36 per cent of

the total number of house sites allotted in the State of Gujarat during the period mentioned above.

The figures presented in the Table 8.1 throw further light on the allotment of house sites to agricultural labourers of different ethnic groups and castes.

TABLE 8.1 Allotment of House Sites to SCs, STs and Others

Sr. No.	Time period	S.C.	S.T.	Others	Total
1.	From the commencement of the scheme until 30-3-1974	43,906	53,031	1,07262	2,04199
2.	1-4-74 to 31-3-78	34,415	33,737	1,03378	1,69530
3.	1-4-78 to 31-3-79	7,558	4,485	14798	26841
4.	1-4-79 to 31-3-80	1,721	1,767	3077	6565
		87,600 21.51%	93,020 22.85%	2,26,515 55.64%	4,07135 100%

Reaction of Recipients of House Sites

After the allotment of the house sites to the bonafide agricultural labourers in different types of villages, the immediate task was to give possession of the plots to the parties concerned. Wherever, surplus plots of land were available around the village site, necessary action was taken to acquire such plots of land by the local authorities. In the villages, where vacant plots of land were not available, the land earmarked for pasture or the land which fell in the category of waste land had to be acquired. For this purpose, the Village Panchayat concerned had to pass a resolution to be forwarded to the Revenue Department of the Government. The Revenue Department took necessary action and in due course of time handed over such plots of land to the Village Panchayat concerned. In some cases, the time lag between sending the resolution by the Village Pachayat to the Revenue Department and the finalisation of decision taken by the government was considerably big. This was one of the reasons why allotment of house sites to the bonafide applicants created certain practical difficulties. In order that such difficulties are taken care of immediately,

special Circle Inspectors were appointed to complete the necessary procedures at taluka level. When this was not done, the usual category of Circle Inspectors took their own time and leisure to demarcate the plots to be handed over to the parties concerned. In fact, it was necessary to have special surveyors to be sent to the villages from the survey department of the Government in order to assist the Circle Inspectors in this work.

The above reasons indicating slackness in administrative action were not the only hurdles in the implementing house site programme. Those who were given the house sites in their name also failed to take necessary action in building their houses in time. Some of those who were in acute need of a house, however, went ahead using the house site for building their residence. Many of those who already had some arrangements for housing did not take immediate steps to built houses on the plot given to them. This means that the very purpose of taking quick action for free of cost plots for house sites to a number of agricultural labourers remained partly fulfilled. There were no doubt certain reasons of under-fulfilment of the real target of building houses at the house sites given free of cost to the agricultural labourers. We shall throw light on some of these points.

(i) The method of selection of some sites by Gram Panchayats was defective. They had passed the resolution and even received the orders from the government to go ahead distributing 100 sq. yards of plots to the bonafide agricultural labourers. There were also cases where the monsoon water was passing through such plots of land. In some other cases, the house sites located were quite far away from the village site and were sometimes located on the bank of tank or river. Some plots of surplus land were used unauthorisedly by some parties from where sites were alloted. Of those who received free gift of unmanagable house sites under such circumstances did not bother to build their houses;

(ii) In some cases, the village panchayat passed the resolution and approached the government for acquiring land near the village without asking the bonafide private landholders to whom it belonged. The original landholders of such plots of land went to the Court of Law to prevent distribution of house sites as a result of which the implementation of the scheme suffered a great deal;

(iii) After the allotment of the plots, those who were not badly in need of building houses immediately did not make any progress in the utilisation of the plots given to them. The slackness in the action to be taken by the allottee of the house sites was also on account of the belief that government will also help them in building the houses on the plots given free of cost to them. On account of the delay in building the houses timely, the wooden posts dividing one plot from the other were wiped out in the monsoon and as a result of which it was difficult to identify clearly which plot of land beloged to whom;

(iv) There were agricultural labourers who worked in the particular village as temporary immigrants. They used to live in temporary huts in villages year after year. When such outside labourers were given free plots of land for house sites in the place of their old huts, they did not bother to make permanant arrangements for their housing facilities; and

(v) In some villages, the immigrant agricultural labourers were already living on rental basis on the land of others. When such people were given plots of land, they did not like to shift their location to another place because they found their older places more suitable. This was more so where they were given regular house sites on the bank of a tank or river where the risk and harassment from rain water and floods were high.

The reasons noted above were not conducive to the successful implementation of the programme of giving house sites to agricultural labourers. Of these difficulties, there were cases of bad environment and difficult locational situations. However, there were other reasons which went against successful implementation of the house site programme. The values, attitude and behaviour of the people, who were not happy with the very idea of this programme, were directly or indirectly oppossed by them. This becomes clear from the following points:

(i) The leaders of some villages, where the agricultural labourers had come from outside the village, were not interested to see that they become bonafide residence of the village. In such villages neither the government nor the immigrant agricultural labourers received cooperation to built house sites.

(ii) In some villages, mischivious persons applied for house sites in the names of minor children. Such applications were largely rejected. While in other cases, non-eligible ones were somehow approved by the Land Committee. When these were oppossed by other villagers, inquiries had to be held as a result of which the programme of giving house sites to the bonafide agricultural labourers was bogged down;

(iii) In some villages, there were applicants who had their houses in other villages or in nearby towns. When applications of such unqualified persons were approved, they were oppossed by others. The local authorities had to take necessary action to reject such applications. This created lot of difficulties in the way of distribution of house sites to the bonafide landless labourers,

(iv) In some other villages, the land which belonged to the government was marked for preparing plots to be given to the landless agricultural labourers. When some of the villagers oppossed the use of government land for this purpose, the whole process of distribution of house sites had to be abandoned. In the case of scheduled castes in some villages, the plots were given far away from the locality where most of them were living before. The allottees of the house sites were not prepared to go away and build their houses in relative isolated and scattered places for lack of safety;

(v) Some of the scheduled castes households who had their own houses and were land owners applied in the name of minor children for allottment of house sites. When such cases were oppossed by the villagers, their applications were rejected and as a result of which a climate of dissatisfaction was created among the scheduled castes agricultural labourers; and

(vi) In some villages bonafide agricultural labourers happily found that the free of cost land given to them was very valuable in view of the location of the village near the town or the roadside. In such cases, the allottees took the liberty to sell away their land to other parties for economic benefit. Such unauthorised selling of house sites were reported in the case of agricultural labourers who came from outside the village.

One can list a number of such problems encountered in the implementing this programme. The government as well as the Land Committee at the taluka level were put to enormous difficulties on account of many unforeseen hurdles. The government had, therefore, to issue from time to time a number of instructions and circulars helpful in meeting various kinds of objections against the implementation of the programme.

There were many other delicate and concealed impediments encountered by the authorities interested in implementing the programme of house sites for SC landless laboureres.

The State Government had, therefore, no alternative, but to pass resolutions and issue necessary orders from time to time to remedy the difficult situations to counter the hurdles. We shall briefly mention the kind of measures taken by the State Government for correcting anomalies in execution of the programme.

(i) The Government circular of 15.7.1972 ordered that unless the cases of alloting house sites in a village are not satisfactorily settled, the plots of land concerned should not be given by auction to anyone;

(ii) The subsequent circular of the government indicated that since all the members of the Land Committee are not able to remain present at the meeting, the Local MLAs, members of Legal Committee for Social Justice, etc., should be included in the same. As the Chairman of this Committee is from the scheduled castes in a village, his inclusion as a member of the Land Committee should be helpful in removing any injustice done to the members of his community;

(iii) The implementation of the programme was not achieved expeditiously and in course of time more and more applicants for house sites were coming forward, it was decided by the State Government that the time limit for acceptance of application be increased. The government circular in this connection permited acceptance of new application though late;

(iv) In the circular dated 15.11.1974, the State Government declared that sympathetic and lenient attitude will be taken in order to sanction house site plots for the members of scheduled castes and scheduled tribes,

(v) When it was brought to the notice of the government that scheduled castes are given house sites away from the village site, it was decided by the government to issue a special order on 15.2.1977 indicating that the scheduled caste members should be allotted house site plots near the village site and in the vicinity of the houses of the high caste members;

(vi) On 24.2.1977, the government issued another circular indicating that the members of the Valmiki (sweeper) community should be given priority in allotment of plots for house sites. The Land Committee, therefore, took special care to see that not a single Valmiki family remained without the allocation of house site;

(vii) In the Government circular dated 1.8.80 it was decided that the Land Committee should instruct the Taluka Development Officer to examine the applications properly because the village Sarpanches were found to be negligant and approved even wrong applications. The government had already issued a circular on

24.2.1977 indicating that the rural artisans also should be allotted house sites. Among these, those artisans who came from the scheduled castes and scheduled tribes community be given priority;

(viii) The government circular dated 6.10.1976 ordered that the bonded labourers who were made free under the act of abolition of bonded labour be also given the benefit of allocation of plots for house sites. In such cases, the Land Committee should take immediate action and see that they were given copies of government order specifying the allotment; and

(ix) Some villages are located in the vicinity of towns and, therefore, there is little scope for surplus land for house sites. In such cases, the government issued a circular on 5.7.1982 indicating the policy of giving 50 sq. yards house sites instead of 100 sq. yrds plots. Following this resolution, the villages in shortage of house sites for agricultural labourers were given 50 sq. yards house sites to applicants.

Assistance for Building Free Houses in General

Right from 1972 when this programme of giving free house sites was started, 2,55,387 households in Gujarat were given the house sites. In the month of December 1976, it was discovered that large number of applicants were given house sites. However, because of several reasons all of the recipients of the house sites were not able to build their houses. One of the reasons was the lack of money with households concerned. The Government of Gujarat had, therefore, passed a resolution on 25-8-1976 to provide loan and other kinds of help to these people. There were 2 types of schemes for this purpose. In the first type of economic assistance, it was decided to help them in making Rs. 1,450 available for building a house. The break-up of money to be received from various sources was as under:

Rs. 1,000	—	Loan from Nationalised Banks
Rs. 150	—	Free labour contribution of the land owner.
Rs. 100	—	The contribution from District Panchayat and Service Cooperative agencies.
Rs. 200	—	Subsidy from the Government.
Rs. 1,450		

In the next type of economc assistance for very poor people, the bank loan was eliminated and instead of a house, a kind of hut worth Rs. 900 was to be built by the house owner. The break-up of money required for this purpose is presented below:

Rs.	400	—	Subsidy from the Government
Rs.	150	—	Free labour contribution of the house owner.
Rs.	250	—	Contribution from District Panchayat and Service Cooperative agencies.
Rs.	100	—	Development grant for levelling land for house building.
Rs.	900		

It was decided that the households with the annual income upto Rs. 2400 should become eligible for the second category of scheme of building huts instead of houses. A number of terms and conditions laid down for use of material etc. in building houses. The government decided that it was necessary to change the pattern of economic assistance in order that better houses could be built by those with relatively higher income. This was conveyed in the government resolution of 18-2-1977 whereby it was possible for a person to build a house with a total expenditure of Rs. 1800.

In course of time, the State Government, through Department of Panchayat Raj, issued a circular on 3-9-1978 indicating that landless labourers can approach Housing & Urban Development Corporation (HUDCO) for getting loans to build a house. Under this scheme, all the beneficiaries of free house sites be eligible to get a loan of Rs. 900 from HUDCO. In a later circular dated 4-5-1979, the Department of Panchayat of the Government of Gujarat passed a resolution saying that a loan of Rs. 1000 per house was availabe to such persons from HUDCO through Gujarat Rural Housing Board. We need not go into the details of the terms and conditions and the procedures involved in making economic assistance to these people for building houses. However, it may be noted that the Gujarat Rural Housing Board, Gandhinagar evolved 3 designs of houses with different specifications costing a total of Rs. 3,000 per house.

When the programme of giving free of cost house sites for building houses to agricultural labourers was initiated in 1972, not much progress was achieved. The reason was that the people who got the plots did not spend money to build the house. This situation was remedied when the District Panchayat and Taluka Panchayat were asked by the government to take up the responsibility of implementing this programme. It is important to note that by 13-1-1980, the total number of houses built under this scheme came to be 1,11,866. Of these, the houses built for the scheduled castes alone came to be 28,073. This means that about 25 per cent of the houses built under this scheme were made available to the housholds of scheduled castes. It may be noted that the percentage of total number of houses built by that time for the households of scheduled tribes came to be 26.00 per cent. The details of houses built under the scheme through economic assistance is presented in the following table:

TABLE 8.2 Houses Built for SCs, STs and Others

Sr. No.	Year	SC	ST	Others	Total
1.	1976-77	6765	5050	9716	21491
2.	1977-78	9342	9410	17770	34522
3.	1978-79	5279	5423	21274	22876
4.	1979-80	6687	11537	14753	39977
Total		28073	29380	54413	111866
		25.09%	26.27%	48.64%	100%

It is significant to note from Table 8.2 that over and above the number of houses built during 1979-80, about 26,897 houses were said to be under construction. At this stage of development of the programme, it was also reported that the Taluka Panchayats took considerable interest in this activity. There were quite a few voluntary agencies which also took part in the promotion of this programme. In the villages where the houses of agricultural labourers were built in the village site area, the Village Panchayat and the Taluka Panchayat saw that the facilities of drinking water, electricity and good roads were made available to these people.

It may be noted that in the earlier stages of this programme, the banks did not easily came forward with loans for building houses. However, when HUDCO started advancing loans through the responsibility of the Taluka and Village Panchayats, the problem of availability of loans was practically solved. It is needless to say that this happened on account of the guarantee given by the State Government and the District Panchayat for recovery of the loans advanced for buildings houses.

Empirical Data on New House Sites in Relation to Traditional Houses

In the earlier pages of this chapter, we tried to present a comprehensive picture of the programme of building house sites in rural Gujarat. There were also references to the special treatment given to members of scheduled castes and scheduled tribes and backward classes on priority basis. In this section, however, we have data on house sites and related issues regarding building of houses by the members of scheduled castes studied during the present survey. They are presented in 7 statistical tables.

The number of households of scheduled castes covered in this study were 240 as said before. It is interesting to note from Table 8.3 that only 62.91 per cent of the households applied for free house sites. In this activity, the District of Ahmedabad stands first where 78.33 per cent of the sample households applied for house sites. Those who did not apply for house sites were 37.08 per cent of the total sample households.

TABLE 8.3 Households of SCs Who Applied for House-site

District	No. of sample H.H.	Those who applied	Those who did not apply
Ahmedabad	60	47 (78.33)	13 (21.66)
Kaira	60	30 (50.00)	30 (50.00)
Mehsana	60	33 (55.00)	27 (45.00)
Surendranagar	60	41 (68.33)	19 (31.66)
Total	240 (100.00)	151 (62.91)	89 (37.08)

The Table 8.4 presents data on the number of households who received house sites and those who did not receive the same, in spite of their efforts to make formal applications. Out of 151 households, who applied for house sites, 45.03 per cent were able to get the house sites while 54.97 per cent were not able to receive house sites. It is interesting to note that in the district of Kaira the difference between recipients of the house sites and those who did not receive was very great. Of the remaining 3, in 2 districts, more than 50 per cent of the applicants were able to get house sites. While in the last one, both the recipients and applicants were almost equal.

Table 8.5 throws light on the problem of time lag in making applications and receiving house sites by 83 households who were not able to get them. It is significant to note that the applications of 49.40 per cent of the households were pending with the authorities without approval for 3 years. The percentage of those whose applications were pending for 4

TABLE 8.4 Recipients of House-sites

District	No. of H.H. applicants for house-sites	Those who received house-sites	Those who did not receive house-sites
Ahmedabad	47	17 (36.17)	39 (63.82)
Kaira	30	22 (73.33)	8 (26.66)
Mehsana	33	10 (30.30)	23 (69.69)
Surendranagar	41	19 (46.34)	22 (53.65)
Total	151 (100.00)	68 (45.03)	83 (54.97)

TABLE 8.5 Time of Pending Applications for House-sites

District	No.of H.H. not receiving house sites	Years of pending application			
		1 year	2 to 3 years	4 to 5 years	more than 5 years
Ahmedabad	30		23 (76.66)	7 (23.33)	—
Kaira	8	—	7 (87.50)	1 (12.50)	—
Mehsana	23	12 (52.17)	6 (26.08)	—	5 (21.73)
Surendranagar	22	—	5 (22.32)	17 (77.27)	—
Total	83 (100.00)	12 (14.45)	41 (49.50)	25 (30.12)	5 (6.02)

to 5 years came to be 30.12 per cent. There were also 6.02 per cent of non-recipients households whose applications were pending for more than 5 years.

We shall now throw light on the reasons why the applications of the 83 households were not accepted in spite of lapse of considerable period of time. Table 8.6 throws light on this subject. It is interesting to note that 34.94 per cent of the households reported that they did not get house sites because Village Panchayat did not have surplus land. There were 19.28 per cent of the households who said that the Village Panchayat did not forward their applications for approval to Taluka Panchayat. It is significant

TABLE 8.6 Reasons of Non-acceptance of Application for House-sites

District	No.of H.H.	Panchayat had no surplus land	Panchayat sent application for approval	Panchayat did not reply	Being land holder on Revenue Record	Application not done in Group
Ahmedabad	30 (100)	7 (23.33)	10 (33.33)	11 (36.37)	2 (6.67)	—
Kaira	8 (100)	—	—	—	—	8 (100.0)
Mehsana	23 (100)	12 (52.17)	4 (17.39)	6 (26.09)	1 (4.35)	—
Surendra-nagar	22 (100)	10 (45.45)	2 (9.09)	1 (4.55)	1 (4.55)	8 (36.36)
Total	83 (100)	29 (34.94)	16 (19.28)	18 (21.69)	4 (4.82)	16 (19.28)

to note that 21.69 per cent of the households said that the Village Panchayats, to whom they approached with applications, did not respond. There were 4.82 per cent of the households who said that they were disqualified from receiving house sites because they were holders of cultivable land on Revenue Records. It is surprising to note that 19.28 per cent of the households indicated that their applications were not considered because they did not apply in the form of a meaningful group.

In Table 8.7, we have data on reasons why those who were allotted

TABLE 8.7 Reasons Why Allotees of House-sites were not Able to Build Houses

District	No.of allotee H.H. who could not build houses	Reasons of not building houses			
		No money for building	Expecting loan from the Govt.	Non-suitable house site	Want of suitable advice and guidance
Ahmedabad	15	1 (6.67)	10 (66.67)	2 (13.33)	2 (13.33)
Kaira	18	—	12 (66.67)	4 (22.22)	2 (11.11)
Mehsana	8	2 (25.00)	4 (50.00)	2 (25.00)	—
Surendranagar	10	2 (20.00)	4 (40.00)	4 (40.00)	—
Total	51 (100.00)	5 (9.80)	30 (58.82)	12 (23.53)	4 (7.84)

house sites were not able to build houses. The number of people who were allotted house sites as indicated earlier were 51. There were 58.82 per cent of the households who said that they were not able to build houses because they expected loans to be received from the Government. There were 23.53 per cent of the households who indicated that they did not build houses because plots given to them were not suitably located. Of the remaining households, 9.80 per cent said that they had no ready money to build houses while 7.84 per cent said that they wanted technical advices and guidance for building houses.

In Table 8.8, we are presenting data on those who were allotted house sites, but were or were not able to build houses. Out of the total of 68 households who received house sites there were 75.00 per cent who were not able to build houses. However, there were 25.00 per cent who built houses.

TABLE 8.8 Allotees of House-sites Who were Able to Build Houses

District	No. of H.H. who received house-sites	Those who could not built houses	Those who built houses
Ahmedabad	17	15 (88.23)	2 (11.76)
Kaira	22	18 (81.81)	4 (18.18)
Mehsana	10	8 (80.00)	2 (20.00)
Surendranagar	19	10 (52.63)	9 (47.36)
Total	68 (100.00)	51 (75.00)	17 (25.00)

In Table 8.9, we have indicated as to how many households built their houses with or without assistance from government. Out of 17 households in this category, there were 82.00 per cent who received assistance from Government sources while 18.00 per cent built houses without such assistance.

In this concluding section we shall present the analysis of empirical data collected during the present survey with regard to traditional houses in which most of the sample households were living. It is important to note that some of the data presented under this general cover may also pertain to a small section of those households who acquired the housing facility under the 20-Point Programme.

TABLE 8.9 Allotees Who Built Houses With or Without Subsidy

District	No. of H.H. who built houses	Those who received Govt. subsidy	Those who did not receive Govt. subsidy
Ahmedabad	2	1 (50.00)	1 (50.00)
Kaira	4	4 (100.00)	-
Mehsana	2	2 (100.00)	-
Surendranagar	9	7 (77.77)	2 (22.22)
Total	17 (100.00)	14 (82.00)	3 (18.00)

In Table 8.10, we present data on sources of acquisition of houses as well as house sites by sample households. Out of 240 sample households, 89.16 per cent inherited their houses. As against this, traditional types of houses, 7.78 per cent of the houses built on house sites received from government. There were also 3.33 per cent of the households who were able to build houses by their own efforts.

TABLE 8.10 Methods of Acquiring Housing Accomodation

District	No. of H.H.	Inherited house	House built on Govt. House-site	House built on personal efforts	Living in rented house
Ahmedabad	60	56 (93.33)	2 (3.33)	2 (3.33)	—
Kaira	60	55 (92.66)	4 (6.66)	1 (1.66)	—
Mehsana	60	53 (88.33)	2 (3.33)	4 (6.66)	1 (1.66)
Surendranagar	60	50 (83.33)	9 (15.00)	1 (1.66)	
Total	240 (100.00)	214 (89.16)	17 (7.78)	8 (3.33)	1 (0.41)

In Table 8.11, we find information regarding special types of colonies in which scheduled castes houses are distributed within boundries of villages concerned. There were 77.00 per cent of the households who

TABLE 8.11 Households Living in Special Category of Colonies

District	No. of sample H.H.	Living together in Harijan colony	Living separately in Valmiki colony	Living in Chamar colony	Living in Vankar colony	Living in Senva colony	Living in mixed caste quarters
Ahmedabad	60	56 (93.33)	—	1 (1.66)	3 (5.00)	—	—
Kaira	60	36 (60.00)	6 (10.00)	12 (20.00)	6 (10.00)	—	—
Mehsana	60	47 ((78.33)	5 (8.33)	4 (6.66)	1 (1.66)	3 (5.00)	—
Surendranagar	60	45 (75.00)	9 (15.00)	1 (1.66)	4 (6.66)	— —	1 (1.66)
Total	240 (100.00)	184 (77.00)	20 (8.33)	18 (7.50)	14 (5.83)	3 (1.25)	1 (0.41)

said that they were living together in specified Harijan Colony in a village irrespective of difference of sub-castes. On the other hand, there were 8.33 per cent houses located in Valmiki Colony, 7.50 per cent in Chamar Colony, 5.83 per cent in Vankar Colony and 1.25 per cent in Senva Colony. This presents an overall situation of distribution of houses of different scheduled castes and sub-castes in sample villages. It is important to note that there is only one household living in a mixed caste housing location.

The data on materials used in building the traditional and other categories of houses are presented in Table 8.12. Here we find that 82.08 per cent of the households owned kutcha houses, while 14.16 per cent households had pucca houses. There were 3.75 per cent of households living in huts of thatch and tin roof houses.

We shall now deal with living spacre facilities available to scheduled castes households. In Table 8.13 are presented the data on the number of rooms available in the houses of these people. Out of 240 sample households, 70.83 per cent had one room houses. This means that a room is a 4 wall enclosure and a suitable roof. There were 26.25 per cent of the houses with 2 rooms, and 2.08 per cent with three rooms while only 0.83 per cent of the houses had 4 room facility.

In Table 8.14, we have data on whether facilities of window in the houses of scheduled castes were available. Out of 240 households, there were 69.58 per cent who had facility to atleast one window in their houses. On the other hand, there were 30.41 per cent households with no facility

TABLE 8.12 Ownership of Houses According to Material Used

District	No. of sample H.H.	Owners of Katcha houses	Owners of Pacca Houses	Owners of houses with Tin roof
Ahmedabad	60	42 (70.00)	16 (26.66)	2 (3.33)
Kaira	60	52 (86.66)	4 (6.66)	4 (6.66)
Mehsana	60	57 (95.00)	3 (5.00)	—
Surendranagar	60	46 (76.66)	11 (18.33)	3 (5.00)
Total	240 (100.00)	197 (82.08)	34 (14.16)	9 (3.75)

TABLE 8.13 Facility of Number of Rooms in Houses

District	No. of sample H.H.	H.H. with One room house	H.H. with Two room house	H.H. with Three room house	H.H. with Four room house
Ahmedabad	60	40 (66.66)	17 (28.33)	2 (3.33)	1 (1.66)
Kaira	60	41 (68.33)	16 (26.66)	3 (5.00)	—
Mehsana	60	47 (78.33)	12 (8.20)	—	1 (1.66)
Surendranagar	60	42 (70.00)	18 (30.00)	—	—
Total	240 (100.00)	170 (70.83)	63 (26.25)	5 (2.80)	2 (0.83)

of window in the houses.

In Table 8.15, we have detailed data on the total number of 167 houses having window facility, we have 71.85 per cent houses with one window, 23.33 per cent with two windows, 1.79 per cent with three windows, 1.19 per cent with four windows, 1.79 per cent with 5 windows.

In Table 8.16, we have data on whether the scheduled castes houses had the facility of bathroom or not. It is interesting to note that out of 240 households, 65.83 per cent had improvised facility for taking bath on a stone slab in the front of the house. There were 26.25 per cent of houses

TABLE 8.14 Houses With and Without Facility of Widows

District	No. of sample H.H.	With facility of windows	Without facility of windows
Ahmedabad	60	44 (73.33)	16 (26.66)
Kaira	60	29 (48.33)	31 (51.66)
Mehsana	60	42 (70.00)	18 (30.00)
Surendranagar	60	52 (86.66)	8 (13.33)
Total	240 (100.00)	167 (69.58)	73 (30.41)

TABLE 8.15 Number of Windows in Houses

District	No.of H.H. with facility of windows	With one window	With two windows	With three windows	With four windows	With five windows
Ahmedabad	44	26 (59.09)	13 (29.54)	2 (4.54)	1 (2.27)	2 (4.54)
Kaira	29	21 (72.41)	6 (20.68)	—	1 (3.44)	1 (3.44)
Mehsana	42	32 (76.19)	10 (23.80)	—	—	—
Surendranagar	52	41 (78.84)	10 (19.23)	1 (1.92)	—	—
Total	167 (100.00)	120 (71.85)	39 (23.35)	3 (1.79)	2 (1.19)	3 (1.79)

whose members were reported to take bath in public tanks or on near by public well. There were 5.0 per cent households who had the facility of taking bath in an enclosed place with or without roof and 2.91 per cent had the facility of improvised bathroom with doors.

In the end, we have in Table 8.17 data on the facility of electricity. This, of course, refers to the households located in the villages where electricity connection was provided. Out of 240 households, there were 30.00 per cent of households with electricity concetions in SC houses while there were 70.00 per cent without the facility of electricity.

TABLE 8.16 Houses With Facility of Bath Rooms

District	No.of sample H.H.	Bathe on stone-slab in front of house	Bathe at any where at well or tank for public	Bathe in an open land enclosed place	Bathe in a simple bath-room with doors
Ahmedabad	60	40 (66.66)	17 (28.33)	1 (1.66)	2 (3.33)
Kaira	60	37 (61.66)	16 (26.66)	4 (6.66)	3 (5.00)
Mehsana	60	45 (75.00)	13 (21.66)	2 (3.33)	-
Surendranagar	60	36 (60.00)	17 (28.33)	5 (8.33)	2 (3.33)
Total	240 (100.00)	158 (65.83)	63 (26.25)	12 (5.00)	7 (2.91)

Table 8.17 Houses With Facility of Electricity

District	No.of sample H.H.	With electric connection	Without electric connection
Ahmedabad	60	23 (38.33)	37 (61.66)
Kaira	60	14 (23.33)	46 (76.66)
Mehsana	60	12 (20.00)	48 (80.00)
Surendranagar	60	23 (38.33)	37 (61.66)
Total	240 (100.00)	72 (30.00)	168 (70.00)

9

LIVELIHOOD FROM AGRICULTURAL LABOUR AND OTHER OCCUPATIONS

Introduction

It has been emphasised earlier in different contexts that a large number of scheduled castes in rural areas depend entirely or partially on agricultural labour for earning livelihood. This is a kind of hangover of the past from which the scheduled castes have not been able to extricate themselves and improve their occupational status in society. After Independence, efforts were made to introduce changes in the occupational pattern, basically exploitative of the labour of scheduled castes and other backward class communities. We have, therefore, collected data also on the members of the scheduled castes who tried to jump over the wall of exploitation and disparity, by entering into more remunerative and socially prestigious occupations. This chapter deals not only with the social position, income, etc., of scheduled castes not only from agricultural labour, but also from animal husbandry, service, cottage industries, trade and miscellaneous occupations.*

Households Engaged in Agricultural Labour

In this section, we present basic information on the number of sample households who were engaged in agricultural labour either as main or subsidiary occupation or in combination with other petty occupations. From Table 9.1, we find that out of the total sample of 240, we had 204

* Prof. T. Nakasato and Prof. H. Yanagiva and their colleagues' study in select & Rural Gujarat, sponsored by Japanese Ministry of Education, has rightly emphasised on diversification of occupations among backward classes for their economic and social betterment. See *The Sunday Times*, 26th November, 1995.

households who had reported to be engaged in agricultural labour as one of the occupations. This shows that 85.00 per cent of the total sample households depended on agricultural labour in contrast to 15.00 per cent of households depending on occupations other than agricultural labour. The overall picture makes it very clear that scheduled castes in rural areas resorted to agricultural labour as the main stay of their life.

In Table 9.2, we have data on working days of households engaged

TABLE 9.1 : Households Engaged in Agricultural Labour

District	Total No. of H.H.	No. of H.H. in agricultural labour	No. of H.H. not doing agricultural labour
Ahmedabad	60	51	9
Kaira	60	51	9
Mehsana	60	55	5
Surendranagar	60	47	13
Total	240	204	36
	(100.00)	(85.00)	(15.00)

in agricultural labour. The number of days available of 204 households for agricultural labour per annum came to be 93,283. This means that the number of agricultural labour days per household came to be 457 only. This indicates that eventhough agricultural labour was the main stay of life for the members of the households, they had to undertake other supporting activities to keep bysy on other days.

TABLE 9.2 : Working Days of those Engaged in Agricultural Labour

District	No. of H.H. in agriculture labour	Availability of total No. of days for agri. labour per annum	No. of agro-labour days per H.H.
Ahmedabad	51	25420	498
Kaira	51	21218	416
Mehsana	55	27170	494
Surendranagar	47	19475	414
Total	204	93283	457

In Table 9.3, we have information on bonded labourers among the scheduled castes. It shows that out of the total sample households, only 1.25 per cent reported that they were working as bonded labourers. This

TABLE 9.3 : Households Working as Bonded Labourers

District	No. of H.H.	Those who said they were bonded labourers	Those who denied that they bonded labourers
Ahmedabad	60	1 (1.67)	59 (98.33)
Kaira	60	1 (1.67)	59 (98.33)
Mehsana	60	1 (1.67)	59 (98.33)
Surendranagar	60	-	60 (100.00)
Total	240 (100.00)	3 (1.25)	237 (98.75)

was just a residual group of people who were treated by their landlords as bonded labourers. This practice was virtually banned by the government. Those who denied that they were bonded labourers were, therefore, 98.75 per cent of the total sample households.

In Table 9.4, we have interesting data presenting the classification of agricultural labourers according to sex and age group. The total number of persons engaged in this occupation was reported to be 603 out of which 314 were males and 287 females. In terms of age and sex of members engaged in this occupation, we find that 267 persons fell in the age group of 15 to 29. The next largest number of agricultural labourers were 175 who fell in age group of 30 to 44. In the third age group of 45 to 59 years we have 115 persons engaged in agricultural labour. It is clear that the younger members of households between the age group of 6 and 14 and the older members from 60 and above were insignificant in the occupation of agricultural labour.

We shall now throw light on the mandays available to agricultural labour by sex in Table 9.5. The overall picture we get from this table shows that 159.82 mandays were available to 314 males per annum to agricultural labour. On the other hand 149.13 mandays per annum were available to SC females doing agricultural labour. The average mandays available to agricultural labourers came to be 154.70 per annum.

Income from Agricultural Labours

In Table 9.6, we present classification of agricultural labourers by sex and the wages earned by them per day. The range of income per day for the

TABLE 9.4 : Agricultural Labourers by Sex and Age-groups

District	Total no. of agricultural labourers			Sexwise Age-groups of Agricultural Labourers														
				6 - 14			15 - 29			30 - 44			45 - 59			60 & above		
	M	F	Total	M	F	Total	M	F	Total	M	F	Total	M	F	Total	M	F	Total
Ahmedabad	96	70	166	2	3	5	46	30	76	14	20	34	25	13	38	9	4	13
Kaira	74	69	143	2	1	3	31	33	64	21	20	41	14	13	27	6	2	8
Mehsana	72	86	158	-	2	2	29	47	76	24	27	51	27	9	26	2	1	3
Surendranagar	72	64	136	5	2	7	24	17	51	26	23	49	14	10	24	3	2	5
Total	314	289	603	9	8	17	130	137	267	89	86	175	70	45	115	20	9	29

TABLE 9.5 : Man-days of Work Available Per Annum to Agricultural Labourers by Sex

District	Male			Female			Total for both sexes		
	No. of Agri. labourers	No. of man-days available	Average per capita	No. of Agri. labourers	No. of Man-days available	Average per capita	No. of Agri. labourers	No. of man-days available	Average per capita.
Ahmedabad	96	15715	163.70	70	9705	138.64	166	25420	153.13
Kaira	74	11228	151.73	69	9990	144.78	143	21218	148.38
Mehsana	72	11970	155.94	86	15200	176.74	158	27170	171.96
Surendranagar	72	11270	156.53	64	8205	128.20	136	19475	143.20
Total	314	50183	159.82	289	43100	149.13	603	93283	154.70

TABLE 9.6 : Agricultural Labourers by Sex Earning Daily Wages

District	No. of Agri. labourers			Variations in wages reveived for per day																							
				Rs.3			Rs.4			Rs.5			Rs.6			Rs.7			Rs.8			Rs.9			Rs.10		
	M	F	Total	M	F	Total	M	F	Total	M	F	Total	M	F	Total	M	F	Total	M	F	Total	M	F	Total	M	F	Total
Ahmedabad	96	70	166	-	1	1	8	10	18	59	47	106	8	3	11	11	5	16	10	4	14	-	-	-	-	-	-
Kaira	74	69	143	-	-	-	-	1	1	26	32	58	20	14	34	18	14	32	-	-	-	-	-	-	10	8	18
Mehsana	72	86	158	5	6	11	4	6	10	14	25	39	27	27	54	12	8	20	4	10	14	3	-	3	3	4	7
Surendranagar	72	64	136	-	-	-	6	4	10	13	15	28	33	29	62	13	7	20	6	7	13	1	1	2	2	1	3
Total	314	289	603	5	7	12	18	21	39	112	119	231	88	73	161	44	44	88	20	21	41	4	1	5	15	13	28

agricultural labourers starts from Rs. 3 and goes up to maximum of Rs. 10 per day. Those who earned Rs. 3 per day were 12 persons of which 7 were females and 5 were males. There were 39 persons earning daily wages of Rs. 4; and among them 18 were males and 21 females. The next largest group of persons earning the daily wage of Rs. 5 was 231, and among these 112 were males and 119 females. Those who earned Rs. 6 per day were 161 in all of these 88 are males and 73 females.

Still in the next group of labourers earning higher wage of Rs. 7, 44 were males and 44 females. The number of persons who got the daily wage of Rs. 8 onwards was negligible as compared to those who earned between Rs. 5 to Rs. 7.

In Table 9.7 we have data on income of households of agricultural labourers. The total income received by 204 households engaged in agricultural labour came to be Rs. 5,19.090.

TABLE 9.7 : Income of Households from Agricultural Labourer

District	No.of H.H.	Annual Total Income for all H.H. Rs.	Annual Income per H.H. Rs.
Ahmedabad	51	138100	2708
Kaira	51	124635	2444
Mehsana	55	142065	2583
Surendranagar	47	114290	2431
Total	204	519090	2545

This means that average income per household of agricultural labourers was only Rs. 2,545 per annum. The same data is given in a different way in Table 9.8 throwing light on whether the income derived

TABLE 9.8 : Principal and Subsidiary Annual Income of Agricultural Labours

Agricultural labourers as per only principal or subsidiary occupation.	No. of H.H.	Total Income per annum	Annual Income per H.H.
Only Agricultural Labour	72	2,21,750	3,080
Principal agricultural labour	73	2,07,200	2,838
Subsidiary agricultural labour	59	90,140	1,544
Total	204	5,19,090	2,545

by the households was principal or subsidiary. It is clear that the only income per household for 72 H.H. from agricultural labour was Rs. 3,080. The next group of households had agricultural inome of Rs. 2,838 as principal occupation. The remaining 59 H.H. had taken up agricultural labour as subsidiary occupation with Rs. 1,545 as income per annum.

In Table 9.9 we present data on income of agricultural labourers according to sex of the workers. In all, there were 314 males engaged in this occupation and their total income was Rs. 2,98,780. This means that the income of male agricultural labourers per capita was Rs. 951. On the other hand, the total number of female agricultural labourers was 289, with total of Rs. 2,20,310 income. This indicates that the income of female agricultural labourers per capita was Rs. 762 only. This obviously is lower than the income per capita of males. Also it is lower than average income of Rs. 860 for both sexes.

In Table 9.10, we have the classification of agricultural labourers income according to sub-castes of scheduled castes. The overall picture shows that the largest number of 94 agricultural labourers came from Vankar community. The total income received by them was Rs. 2,42,725. The other sub-castes relatively engaged more in agricultural labour was Chamar whose 63 members derived the annual income of Rs. 1,56,745. The total number of Valmik sub-caste engaged in agricultural labour was 31 with the total income of Rs. 80,650 only. It is interesting to note that the members of other sub-castes such as Garoda, Senva, Barot, Turi, etc., were not significantly engaged in agricultural labour.

In Table 9.11, we present data on income of agricultural labourers according to whether it was the only occupation of the household, and whether it was principal or subsidiary occupation. The number of households who reported that agricultural labour was the only occupation were 72. The total income of these group of households was Rs. 2,21,750, which came to be Rs. 3,080 per household. The income of those who had taken this occupation as the principal one,but not the only one, were 73. The total income of this group of people was Rs. 2,07,200. It means that the income per household in this group came to be Rs. 2,839. There were 59 households who had agricultural labour as their subsidiary occupation. The total income of this group came to be Rs. 90,140 and the income per household was Rs. 1,528.

In Table 9.12, we have a consolidated picture of the income of households engaged in agricultural labour as only or principal occupation. There were in all 145 households in this composite category. The total income of this group of people from agricultural labour was Rs. 4,28,950. However, they also,earned income from other occupations which amounted

TABLE 9.9 : Income of Agricultural Labourers by Sex

District	Male			Female			Total		
	No. of male agricultural labourers	Total income in Rs.	Per Capita income in Rs. p.a.	No. of Female agri. labourers	Total Income in Rs. p.a.	Per Capita Income in Rs. p.a.	Total No. of agri. labourers	Total Income in Rs. p.a.	Average per Capita income Rs. p.a.
Ahmedabad	96	88315	919	70	49785	711	166	138100	832
Kaira	74	70395	951	69	54240	786	143	124635	871
Mehsana	72	75275	1045	86	66790	776	158	142065	899
Surendranagar	72	64795	899	64	49495	773	136	114290	840
Total	314	298780	951	289	220310	762	603	519090	860

TABLE 9.10 : Agricultural Labourers' Income by SC Sub-castes

District	Name of sub-casts engaged in agricultural labour													
	Vankar		Chamar		Valmik		Garoda		Senva		Barot/Turi and others		Total	
	No. of H.H.	Income Rs. p.a.	No. of H.H.	Income Rs. p.a.	No. of H.H.	Income Rs. p.a.	No. of H.H.	Income Rs. p.a.	No. of H.H.	Income Rs. p.a.	No. of H.H.	Income Rs. p.a.	No. of H.H.	Income Rs. p.a.
Ahmedabad	25	68605	17	40555	2	7750	2	5170	3	9900	2	6120	51	138100
Kaira	16	31895	18	49630	14	37550	3	5830	-	-	-	-	51	124635
Mehsana	23	68815	21	51940	6	11760	-	-	5	9550	-	-	55	142065
Surendranagar	30	73410	7	14890	9	23590	1	2400	-	-	-	-	47	114290
Total	94	242725	63	156745	31	80650	6	13400	8	19450	2	6120	204	519090

TABLE 9.11: Income of Agricultural Labourers by Principal and Subsidiary Occupation

District	Income from agricultural labour alone			Income from agricultural labour as principal			Income from agricultural labour as subsidiary			Total Income from agricultural labour		
	No.of H.H.	Income in Rs. p.a.	Per H.H. income Rs. p.a.	No.of H.H.	Income in Rs. p.a	Per H.H. income Rs. p.a.	No.of H.H.	Incoe in Rs. p.a.	Per H.H. income Rs. p.a.	No.of H.H.	Income Rs. p.a.	Per H.H. income Rs. p.a.
Ahmedabad	20	61610	3081	22	64730	2943	9	12760	1307	51	138100	2708
Kaira	20	63550	3171	18	42665	2371	13	18420	1417	51	124635	2444
Mehsana	19	47060	2477	20	67565	3379	16	27440	1715	55	142065	2583
Surendranagar	13	49530	3810	13	32240	2480	21	32520	1549	47	114290	2432
Total	72	221750	3080	73	207200	2839	59	90140	1528	204	519090	2545

to a total of Rs. 1,07,102 per annum. The consolidated income of the whole group was Rs. 5,36,052 and the average income per household was Rs. 3,697.

TABLE 9.12: Income of Households from Agricultural Labour as Principal Occupation

District	No.of H.H.	Income from Agricultural labour only or principal Rs. p.a.	Income from other occupation Rs. p.a.	Consolidated Income Rs. p.a.	Average income per household p.a.
Ahmedabad	42	126340	25713	142053	3621
Kaira	38	106215	24653	130868	3444
Mehsana	39	114625	37014	151639	3889
Surendranagar	26	81770	19722	101492	3904
Total	145	428950	107102	536052	3697

In Table 9.13, we have data giving a consolidated picture of mandays and income available to agricultural labourers. Out of the total of 603 persons engaged in this occupation, the mandays available to them for work came to be 93,283 and the total income received by them came to be Rs. 5,19,090. The annual mandays available for households were 457 and the income per household came to be Rs. 2,544. In the end it may be noted that the average mandays per capita turned out to be 154 for which the average income per capita was Rs. 861.

Households Engaged in Animal Husbandry

One of the contributory occupations on which the scheduled castes households depend in absence of sufficient land for cultivation is animal husbandry. In this general category, we have included also the occupation of poultry farming. It has, however, not been possible to present separate data on poultry farming because it was not so vigorously pursued by the scheduled castes households for earning additional income.

In Table 9.14, we have basic data indicating number of households with or without cattle or poultry. Out of 240 sample households, 118 HH or 49.17 per cent, had cattle or poultry with them. On the other hand, there were 50.83 per cent or 122 households who were devoid of cattle or poultry. In the next Table 9.15, we present data giving the number and value of different kinds of cattle owned by 118 households. There were 10 households having 13 cows worth Rs. 18,400. Leaving aside the stud bull and young ones of the cows which were not reported in large number, we have data on the number of oxen in possession of the households. There were 32 households in possession of 55 oxen costing Rs. 66,300. The

TABLE 9.13: Man-days of Work and Income Per Annum Available to Agricultural Labourers

District	Total No.of H.H.	No.of H.H. doing agri. labour	No.of persons doing agri. labour	Total man-days available for agri. labour	Total Income from Agri-labour Rs. p.a.	Man-days available per H.H.	Income per H.H. Rs. p.a.	Average Man-days available per capita	Average Income per capita Rs. p.a
Ahmedabad	60	51	166	25420	138100	498	2707	153	831
Kaira	60	51	143	21218	128635	416	2444	148	871
Mehsana	60	55	158	27170	142065	495	2583	171	899
Surendranagar	60	47	136	19475	114290	414	2432	143	840
Total	240	204	603	93283	519090	457	2544	154	861

TABLE 9.14 Households With or Without Cattle and Poultry

District	Total No.of H.H.	H.H.owning cattle-head or poultry	H.H. having no cattle-head or poultry
Ahmedabad	60	28	32
Kaira	60	23	37
Mehsana	60	33	37
Surendranagar	60	34	26
Total	240 100.00	118 49.17%	122 50.83%

important milch animal next to cow is buffalos and we have here 62 households owning 72 buffalos worth Rs. 1,56,000. The number of young ones of buffalo owned by 34 households were in all 42, costing Rs. 12,350. The number of goats were owned by 50 households. These households had 76 goats worth Rs. 13,410. There was only one household owning two sheep worth Rs. 200. None of the households had horse, camel, or donkey. There was only one household in possession of poultry with 150 birds worth Rs. 1,500. This means that two households were in possession of 152 poultry plus other animals worth Rs. 1700 in all.

In Table 9.16, we have data indicating whether all the households, who possessed cattle or poultry, were doing business of selling the produce. Out of 240 households, there were only 82 households engaged in the business of animal husbandry. While the remaining 158 did not earn income from cattle or poultry.

In Table 9.17, we have data on the ownership of cow and use of milk derived by the households concerned. There were 10 households owning 13 cows. The total yield per annum in litres was 8,560. This means that yield of milk per household was, 856 litres and the same per cow was 658 litres. The households used 2100 litres of milk for domestic consumption which amounted to 210 litres per household. The total amount of milk sold per year for all the households came to be, worth Rs. 6,460, which amounted to only 646 litres of milk sold by households per year.

In Table 9.18, we have data on the number of households owning buffalo and the supply of milk. There were 62 households owning 72 buffalos giving the yield of 63,350 litres. The milk yield per household was 990 litres and milk yield per buffalo was 852 litres. The households used 16,368 litres of milk for domestic consumption which amounted to 264 litres per household. The total milk of buffalos sold by all the 62 households came to be 44,982 litres and the sale of milk per household was

TABLE 9.15: Value of Cattle and Poultry Owned by Households.

District	Total No. of HH	Cow			Studbul			Young ones of cows			Oxen			Buffalo			Young ones of buffalo			Goat			Sheep Poultry			Horse, camel, donkey		
		HH	CH	Rs.	HH	CH	Rs.	HH	CH	Rs.	HH	CH	Rs.	HH	CH	Rs.	HH	CH	Rs.	HH	CH	Rs.	HH	CH	Rs.	HH	CH	Rs
Ahmeda-bad	28	4	4	1500	2	2	3700	3	3	500	11	18	30800	12	16	34600	8	9	2700	11	15	1750	2	152	1700	-	-	-
Kaira	23	-	-	-	-	-	-	-	-	-	4	7	11000	17	18	36100	2	2	400	5	6	1400	-	-	-	-	-	-
Mehsana	33	2	4	8200	-	-	-	1	1	700	7	9	11200	26	31	66300	17	23	6950	11	20	4000	-	-	-	-	-	-
Surendra-nagar	34	4	5	8700	2	2	2700	5	5	2700	10	21	13300	7	7	19000	7	8	2300	23	35	6260	-	-	-	-	-	-
Total	118	10	13	18400	4	4	6400	9	9	3300	32	55	66300	62	72	156000	34	42	12350	50	76	13410	2	152	1700	-	-	-

Key : HH :Households

CH :Cattlehead

TABLE 9.16: Households Engaged in Business of Animal Husbandry and Poultry

District	Total No.of H.H.	No. of H.H. engaged in the business	No.of H.H. not engaged in the business
Ahmedabad	60	15	45
Kaira	60	15	45
Mehsana	60	27	33
Surendranagar	60	25	35
Total	240	82	158

TABLE 9.17: Ownership of Cows and Use of Milk by Households

District	No.of H.H. owning cows	No.of cows	Total milk yield in litres	Milk yield per H.H. and per cow in litres.		Milk used for domestic purposes.		Milk sold in litres	
				Milk per HH	Milk Per Cow	Milk in lit.	Milk per HH	Milk in lit.	Milk per HH
Ahmedabad	4	4	960	240	240	800	200	160	40
Kaira	-	-	-	-	-	-	-	-	-
Mehsana	2	4	5900	2950	737	300	150	5600	2800
Surendranagar	4	5	1700	425	340	1000	250	700	175
Total	10	13	8560	856	658	2100	210	6460	646

726 litres.

In Table 9.19, we have data on the number of goats and yield of milk received by the households. It is significant to note that there were 50 households owning 76 goats. The total yield of milk in litres per year was 5224. The milk yield per household was 104 litres and so the milk per goat was 69 litres. The overall use of goats milk for domestic purpose was 4654 litres per annum and use per households was 93 litres. The milk sold in the market was only 570 litres per annum which came to be 11 litres per household.

Income from Animal Husbandry

In Table 9.20, we have overall data on the income of 82 households doing business in animal husbandry. The total income of all these households per annum came to be Rs. 1,03,970. This means that the income per household from animal husbandry was Rs. 1268 only. In Table 9.21, we have presented details of income, expenditure etc. of households engaged

TABLE 9.18: Ownership of Buffaloes and Use of Milk by Households

District	No.of H.H. owning buffalo	No.of buffalo	Total milk yield in litres	Milk yield per H.H. and per baffalo in litres.		Milk used for domestic purposes.		Milk sold in litres	
				Milk per H.H.	Milk per head	Milk in lit.	Milk per H.H	Milk in Lit.	Milk per H.H.
Ahmedabad	12	16	8400	700	525	2100	175	6300	525
Kaira	17	18	20410	1201	1134	6030	355	14380	846
Mehsana	26	31	23960	924	773	5868	226	18092	696
Surendranagar	7	7	8580	1226	1226	2370	339	6210	887
Total	62	72	61350	990	852	16368	264	44982	726

TABLE 9.19: Goats owned by Households and Use of Milk

District	No.of H.H. owning goats	No.of goats	Total milk yield in litres	Milk yield per H.H. and per goat in litres		Milk used for domestic purpose		Milk sold in litres	
				Milk per H.H.	Milk per head	Milk in lit.	Milk per H.H	Milk in Lit.	Milk per H.H
Ahmedabad	11	15	780	71	52	750	68	30	3
Kaira	5	6	150	30	25	150	30	-	-
Mehsana	11	20	614	65	31	494	41	120	11
Surendranagar	23	35	3680	160	105	3260	142	420	19
Total	50	76	5224	104	69	4654	93	570	11

TABLE 9.20: Income of Households from Animal Husbandry and Poultry

District	No.of H.H. in the business.	Total annual Income from animal husbandry and poultry Rs.	Annual Income per H.H. Rs.
Ahmedabad	15	17,698	1180
Kaira	15	22,060	1471
Mehsana	27	40,564	1502
Surendranagar	25	23,648	946
Total	82	1,03,970	1268

in the business of animal husbandry. There were in all 82 households doing business of animal husbandry and poultry as indicated earlier. The total income of all these households was Rs. 2,13,151 which amounted to an average income of Rs. 2,599 per annum per household. The expenditure incurred by all the households in the business was reported to be Rs. 1,09,181 which amounted to be the expenditure of Rs. 1,331 per household. This means that the net income derived from animal husbandry by 82 households was Rs. 1,03,970 and the average net income per household was Rs. 1,268. In the end, it may be noted that the output of animal husbandry used for domestic purpose was worth Rs. 57,209 and the out-put sold in cash came to be Rs. 46,761.

In Table 9.22, we have data throwing light on the income of sub-castes of scheduled castes from animal husbandry and poultry. There were 42 households of Vankar group deriving income of Rs. 61,462 per annum from animal husbandary. There were 27 households of Chamar having income of Rs. 36,875 per annum. There were 9 households of Valmik, one of Garoda and 3 of Senva deriving income per annum worth Rs. 4,037, Rs. 216 and Rs. 1,380 respectively. The Table 9.23 throws light on the comparative figures of income from animal husbandry pursued by the households whether as principal or as subsidiary occupation. There were no households deriving income from animal husbandary as the only occupation. Those engaged in animal husbandry as principal occupation were 12 households. they earned annually Rs. 32,700 which amounted to Rs. 2,725 per household. There were 70 households who did animal husbandry as subsidiary occupation. Their annual income was Rs. 91,270 which amounted to Rs. 1,019 per household per annum. The same data presented in Table 9.23 have been recast in Table 9.24 according to the degree of dependence of households on animal husbandry as an important occupation.

In Table 9.25, we have consolidated figures throwing light on the income of households engaged in animal husbandry as principal occupation. The 12 households who came into the group, were deriving Rs. 32,700 from animal husbandry as principal occupation. Their income from other occupations amounted to the total of Rs. 27,093. The consolidated income of all these households per annum was Rs. 59,793 and income per annum per household was Rs. 4,983.

Households Engaged in Cottage Industries

According to the ancient tradition of village India, members of the scheduled castes used to pursue cottage industries involving different

TABLE 9.21: Income and Expenditure, from Animal Husbandry and Poultry

District	No.of H.H.doing business in cattle & Poultry	Total income through the output		Expenditure on cattle and poultry		Net Income in Rs.		Output used of domestic purpose in Rs.		Output sold in Rs.	
		Total Rs. p.a.	Average per H.H.	Total Rs. p.a.	Average per H.H.	Total Rs. p.a.	Average per H.H.	Total Rs. p.a.	Average per H.H.	Total Rs. p.a.	Average per H.H.
Ahmedabad	15	42665	2844	24767	1615	17698	1179	8380	558	9318	621
Kaira	15	56610	3774	34550	2303	22060	1470	16565	1104	5495	366
Mehsana	27	78055	2890	31491	1166	44564	1650	17384	643	23180	858
Surendranagar	25	36021	1440	12373	494	23648	945	14880	595	8768	350
Total	82	213151	2599	109181	1331	103970	1268	57209	698	46761	570

TABLE 9.22: Income from Animal Husbandry and Poultry by SC Sub-castes.

District	Vankar		Chamar		Valmik		Garoda		Senva		Total		Income per H.H.
	No.of H.H.	Income in Rs. p.a.	No.of H.H.	Income in Rs. p.a.	No.of H.H.	Income in Rs. p.a.	No. of H.H.	Income in Rs. p.a.	No. of H.H.	Income in Rs. p.a.	No.of H.H.	Income in Rs. p.a.	Rs. p.a.
Ahmedabad	12	14808	2	2830	1	60	-	-	-	-	15	17698	1179.87
Kaira	6	8355	7	12105	2	1600	-	-	-	-	15	22060	1490.67
Mehsana	11	21909	12	16850	1	425	-	-	3	1380	27	40564	1502.37
Surendranagar	13	16390	6	5090	5	1952	1	216	-	-	25	23648	945.96
Total	42	61462	27	36875	9	4037	1	216	3	1380	82	103970	1267.93

* Barot, Turi and the rest were not engaged in animal husbandry.

TABLE 9.23: Income from Animal Husbandry as Principal and Subsidiary Occupation

District	Annual Income from animal husbandry as principal			Annual income from animal husbandry as subsidiary			Total Income from animal husbandry		
	No. of H.H.	Income in Rs.	Income per H.H.	No. of H.H.	Income in Rs.	Income per H.H.	No. of H.H.	Income in Rs.	Income per H.H.
Ahmedabad	2	6880	3440	13	10818	833	15	17698	1180
Kaira	3	8325	2775	12	13735	1145	15	22060	1471
Mehsana	4	9335	2334	23	31229	7808	27	40564	1503
Surendranagar	3	8160	2720	22	15488	2213	25	23648	946
Total	12	32700	2725	70	71270	1019	82	103970	1268

TABLE 9.24: Income from Animal Husbandry and Poultry as Principal and Subsidiary Occupations

Category of H.H. by occupation	No.of H.H.	Income from animal husbandry or poultry Rs. p.a.	Income per H.H. Rs. p.a.
Income from animal husbandry & poultry only	—	—	—
Income from animal husbandry and poultry as principal occupation	12	32,700	2725
Income from animal husbandry and poultry as subsidiary occupation	70	71,270	1018
Total	82	1,03,970	1268

TABLE 9.25: Income from Animal Husbandry as Principal Occupation

District	No.of H.H.	Income from animal husbandry as principal Rs. p.a.	Income from other occupations Rs. p.a.	Consolidated Income Rs. p.a.	Income per H.H. Rs. p.a.
Ahmedabad	2	6880	5064	11944	5972
Kaira	3	8325	4495	12820	4274
Mehsana	4	9335	10306	19641	4911
Surendranagar	3	8160	7228	15388	5130
Total	12	32700	27093	59793	4983

types of handicrafts based on local materials such as cotton, bamboo, reed, wood, animal hyde, etc. There had been different phases of rise and down fall of traditional art and crafts, which were largely helpful in earning livelihood to the people engaged in cottage industries. One of the very outstanding cottage industries for which the scheduled castes all over India are famous has been weaving. The handloom industry is a hereditary form of art and craft and the means of subsistence for large number of scheduled castes people called the Vankar in Gujarat. Let us see what is the present position of cottage industries in the life of scheduled castes households studied in this survey.

From Table 9.26, we find that out of 240, there were 18.75 per cent of the households engaged in cottage industries. The remaining 81.25 per cent depended on other occupations for earning livelihood. This was a unique situation from what obtained in the historical past of these people.

TABLE 9.26: Households Dependent on Cottage Industry

District	No.of H.H.	H.H.with cottage industry	H.H. not engaged in cottage industry
Ahmedabad	60	10	50
		(16.67)	(83.33)
Kaira	60	5	55
		(8.33)	(91.67)
Mehsana	60	9	51
		(15.00)	(85.00)
Surendranagar	60	21	39
		(35.00)	(65.00)
Total	240	45	195
	(100.00)	(18.75)	(81.25)

In Table 9.27, we have presented the classification of the members of the households engaged in cottage industries by sex and age groups. The maximum number of scheduled castes persons including males and females engaged in cottage industries fall in the age group of 15 to 44 years. There were in all 48 persons out of which males and females were distributed almost in equal number. The total picture shows that out of 70 persons engaged in cottage industries, 58.75 per cent were males and 41.43 per cent females.

The data presented in Table 9.28 indicates that the total income of 45 households engaged in cottage industries was Rs. 98,525 per annum. This means that the overall income per annum per household was Rs. 2,189.

TABLE 9.27: Household Members Engaged in Cottage Industry

District	Sex and age-groups												Total		
	15—29			30—44			45—59			60 & above					
	M	F	Total	M	F	Total	M	F	Total	M	F	Total	M	F	Total
Ahmedabad	4	4	8	1	-	1	3	1	4	1	1	2	9	6	15
Kaira	-	1	1	2	-	2	3	1	4	-	-	-	5	2	7
Mehsana	2	2	4	3	1	4	4	-	4	-	-	-	9	3	12
Surendranagar	2	9	11	11	6	17	5	3	8	-	-	-	18	18	36
Total	8	16	24	17	7	24	15	5	20	1	1	2	41	29	70
	(33.33)	(66.67)	(100)	(70.83)	(29.17)	(100)	(75.00)	(25.00)	(100)	(50.00)	(50.00)	(100)	(58.57)	(41.4)	(100)

TABLE 9.28: Income of Households Engaged in Cottage Industry

District	No.of H.H.	Income Rs.	Income per H.H. Rs.
Ahmedabad	10	11300	1130
Kaira	5	14575	2915
Mehsana	9	11825	1313
Surendranagar	21	60825	2896
Total	45	98525	2189

Table 9.29 presents data throwing light on the income of various sub-castes of scheduled castes, derived from cottage industry. Out of 45 sample households engaged in this profession, we have 40.00 per cent households from Vankar family with total annual income of Rs. 51,515. This sub-caste has been the traditional group of people engaged in weaving. The next group of Chamar have 16 households with total annual income of Rs. 25,050. There were 9 households of Valmik community earning the total income of Rs. 18,260 per annum from cottage industry.

There were only 2 households of Garoda who pursued this profession and earned Rs. 3,700 per annum. It is significant to note that Senva, Barot, Turi etc. were not reported to be engaged in cottage industry.

In Table 9.30, we find income of sample households from cottage industries as principal only and as subsidiary occupation. There was only one household earning Rs. 3,000 per annum from cottage industry. Those who received income from cottage industry as principal occupation were 15 households earning annually Rs. 65,625. The income of this group per household was Rs. 4375. There were 29 households pursuing cottage industry as subsidiary occupation. They earned annually Rs. 29,900 which came to be Rs. 1,032 per household.

In Table 9.31, we have data on consolidated income of households who reported that they were doing cottage industry as the principal occupation. The total number of households in this group was 15 and they earned Rs. 65,625 per annum. The income that they derived from other occupations came to be Rs. 27,066 annually. The consolidated income of these 15 families was Rs. 92,691 which means that a family in this group earned annually Rs. 6179 from cottage industries.

Table 9.32, presents the data on income from cottage industry according to whether it was the only, principal or subsidiary occupation of the household concerned. The figures giving the overall picture are identical with those presented in Table 9.29.

TABLE 9.29: Income of SC Sub-castes from Cottage Industry

District	sub-castes of scheduled castes									
	Vankar		Chamar		Valmik		Garoda		Total	
	No.of H.H.	Income Rs. p.a.	No.of H.H.	Income Rs. p.a.	No.of H.H.	Income Rs. p.a.	No.of H.H.	Income Rs. p.a.	No. of H.H.	Income p.a.
Ahmedabad	6	8600	3	200	-	-	1	700	10	11300
Kaira	-	-	3	5375	1	6200	1	3000	5	14575
Mehsana	1	2500	6	5875	2	3450	-	-	9	11825
Surendranagar	12	40415	4	11800	6	8610	-	-	21	60825
Total	18 (40.00)	51515	16 (35.56)	25050	9 (20.00)	18260	2 (4.44)	3700	45 (100.00)	98525

* Senva, Barot, Turi and the rest were not engaged in cottage industry.

TABLE 9.30: Income of Households from Cottage Industry in Districts as Principal and Subsidiary Occupation

District	Annual income from cottage-industry alone			Annual income from animal husbandry as principal			Annual income from animal husbandry as subsidiary			Total annual income from cottage-industry		
	No.of H.H.	Total Rs.	Per HH Rs.	No.of H.H.	Total Rs.	Per HH Rs.	No.of H.H.	Total Rs.	Per HH Rs.	No.of H.H.	Total Rs.	Per HH Rs.
Ahmedabad	-	-	-	1	2200	2200	9	9100	1012	10	11300	1130
Kaira	1	3000	3000	3	10275	3425	1	1300	1300	5	14575	2915
Mehsana	-	-	-	3	6450	2150	6	5375	896	9	11825	1314
Surendranagar	-	-	-	8	46700	5838	13	14125	1087	21	60825	2897
Total	1	3000	3000	15	65625	4375	29	29900	1032	45	98525	2190

TABLE 9.31: Income of Households having Cottage Industry as Principal Occupation

District	No.of H.H.	Income from cottage industry principal Rs	Income from other occupation Rs	Consolidated Income Rs	Average Income per Household Rs.
Ahmedabad	1	2200	455	2655	2655
Kaira	4	12275	4700	16975	4244
Mehsana	2	4450	2600	7050	3525
Surendranagar	8	46700	19311	66011	8252
Total	15	65625	27066	92691	6179

TABLE 9.32: Income of Households with Cottage Industry as Principal or Subsidiary Occupation

Cottage Industries as per only, principal or subsidiary occupation	No.of H.H.	Income from cottage industry Rs.	Income per H.H. Rs.
Only Service	1	3000	3000
Principal Service	15	65625	4375
Subsidiary Service	29	29900	1032
Total	45	98525	2190

Households Engaged in Trade and Commerce

At this point of time, in the social history of our country, to expect the members of the scheduled castes to be engaged in trade or commerce is nothing but begging the question. The number of thsoe doing trade or business being less than 10 only the data are presented in descriptive form and not were in tabulated form for obvious reasons.

There were only 6 households who reported that they were engaged in trade or commerce for earning livelihood. They were (2.50 per cent) only of the total sample households of 240. The remaining 234 (97.50 per cent) of the households were not engaged in trade or commerce. Those engaged in trade or commerce by sex and age group, were only 6 males and most of them fell in the age group between 30 and 60 years.

The annual income of the members of the 6 households from trade and commerce was Rs. 12,900. This means that the income per household from trade and commerce was Rs. 2,150 per annum. This is almost equal to the income per household of those engaged in cottage industry as indicated earlier.

There were no households of Valmik, Garoda, Senva and others who were engaged in trade or commmerce. There were 5 households of Vankar earning the total income of Rs. 9,900 per annum and only one household of Chamar earned total income of Rs. 3,000 from trade and Commerce.

The data on income of households having trade and commerce as the only principal or subsidiary occupation indicated that the total income of 6 households from trade and commerce was Rs. 12,900 and the income per household was Rs. 2,150. There were only 2 out of 6 households in this category who received total income of Rs. 6,000 per annum from trade and commerce. Their income from other occupations came to be Rs. 1,625 per annum. The consolidated total income of the two households was Rs. 7,625 and income per household was Rs. 3,813.

Households Engaged in Different Types of Services

One who is acquainted with the position of the scheduled castes in rural areas, is aware that there was hardly any scope for employment of scheduled castes in paid service. The scope of employment of some educated and trained scheduled castes persons has no doubt improved now to some extent because of jobs available in the developmental programmes of the government agencies, private organisations, industries, etc.

Out of 240 sample households, there were 14.58 per cent of the households from where at least one member each was engaged in gainful service. This can be seen from Table 9.33. The number of households who reported that no one of their family members was going for service came to be 85.42 per cent of the total sample.

TABLE 9.33: Households Dependent on Service for Livelihood

District	No.of H.H.	H.H. with service men	H.H. without a person in service
Ahmedabad	60	7	53
Kaira	60	12	48
Mehsana	60	10	50
Surendranagar	60	6	54
Total	240 (100.00)	35 (14.58)	205 (85.42)

Table 9.34 gives classification of households by sub-castes receiving income from service. There were 14 households of Vankar earning only Rs. 1,25,236 per annum from service. This was the highest number in all the sub-castes doing service. There were 9 Chamar, 4 Valmik and 6

TABLE 9.34: Income of SC Sub-castes from Service

District	Sub-castes of Scheduled Castes											
	Vankar		Chamar		Valmik		Garoda		Senva		Total	
	No.of H.H.	Rs.	No.of H.H.	Rs.	No.of H.H.	Rs.	No.of H.H.	Rs.	No.of H.H.	Rs.	No.of H.H.	Rs
Ahmedabad	3	31000	3	3000	-	-	1	1200	-	-	7	35200
Kaira	3	33236	3	9840	2	3614	4	26200	-	-	12	72890
Mehsana	5	43800	3	28800	-	-	-	-	2	2400	10	75000
Surendranagar	3	17200	-	-	2	8225	1	4000	-	-	6	29425
Total	14	125236	9	41640	4	11839	6	31400	2	2400	35	212515

* Barot, Turi and the rest were not engaged in service.

TABLE 9.35: Income of Households in Districts for Service as Principal and Subsidiary Occupation

District	No.of H.H.	Income from service alone		No.of H.H.	Income from service as principal		No.of H.H.	Income from service as subsidiary		No.of H.H.	Total income from service	
		Total Rs.	Per H.H. Rs.		Total Rs.	Per H.H. Rs.		Total Rs.	Per H.H. Rs.		Grand Total Rs.	Per H.H. Rs.
Ahmedabad	2	15900	7950	3	15100	5034	2	4200	2100	7	35200	5029
Kaira	2	19536	9768	7	51302	7329	3	2052	684	12	72890	6095
Mehsana	1	9600	9600	7	64200	9172	2	1200	600	10	75000	7500
Surendranagar	1	9000	9000	4	20225	5057	1	200	200	6	29425	4085
Total	6	54036	9006	21	150827	7183	8	7652	957	35	212515	6072

Garoda members from respective households doing service. Their annual income turned out to be Rs. 41,640 Rs. 11,839 and Rs. 31,400 respectively for the sub-castes mentioned earlier. There were only two Senva families who were in service earning annually Rs. 2,400 only.

In Table 9.35, we have data on income of households from service as principal only or subsidiary occupation. There were 6 households whose members earned Rs. 54,036 annually as the only income for livelihood. There were 21 households whose principal dependence for subsistence was service and they earned in all, Rs. 1,50,827. Those who did service as subsidiary occupation were 8 members from the same number of households who annually earned a total of Rs. 7652. The average income of the households for all different groups came to be Rs. 6,072.

The data presented in Table 9.36 were identical with the information presented in terms of importance of the service in the maintenance of the households.

TABLE 9.36: Income of Households from Service as Principal or Subsidiary Occupation

Service as per only. principal or subsidiary occupation	No.of H.H.	Income from service Rs.	Income per H.H. Rs.
Only service	6	54036	9006
Principal service	21	150827	7183
Subsidiary service	8	7652	957
Total	35	212515	6072

Table 9.37 presents consolidated figures on the income of households engaged in service as principal occupation. There were 22 households in this composite group earning Rs. 2,04,863 from service annually. The income of the households from other occupations came to be Rs. 61,136.

TABLE 9.37: Income of Households having Service as Principal Occupation

District	No.of H.H.	Income from service principal Rs.	Income from other occupations Rs.	Consolidated Income Rs.	Average income per Household Rs
Ahmedabad	5	31000	11515	42515	8503
Kaira	9	70838	19280	90188	10021
Mehsana	8	73800	24715	98515	12315
Surendranagar	5	29225	5556	34781	6957
Total	27	204863	61136	265999	9852

The average income per household was Rs. 9,852.

In Table 9.38, we have data indicating whether those who were in service had permanent or temporary jobs. There were in all 39 household members who reported that they were in service. Of these, 87.17 per cent were in permanent service while 12.82 per cent reported that they had temporary service. At the time of the survey of this report, all these 5 persons were not actually on the job. However, we have clubbed them together with the 39 persons with jobs so that we have a total picture of

TABLE 9.38: Persons in Permanent and Temporary Service

District	No.of persons in service	Permanent service	Temporary service
Ahmedabad	7	4 (57.14)	3 (42.85)
Kaira	13	13 (100.00)	-
Mehsana	13	11 (84.61)	2 (15.38)
Surendranagar	6	6 (100.00)	-
Total	39 (100.00)	34 (87.17)	5 (12.82)

the types of services available to them through different channels.

In Table 9.39, we present data on those who were in service, by sex and age. Out of 39 scheduled castes persons who were in service, 17 and 16 each fell in the age group of 15 to 29 and 30 to 44 respectively. All these 33 members in service were males and even the remaining 5 persons in next age group were also males. It is significant to note that there was no female member from sample households engaged in service.

In Table 9.40, we have data on the manner in which all the 39 persons who reported of being in service had jobs. There were 74.35 per cent of the total members in service who said that they got jobs of their own efforts. Those who got jobs through employment exchange services were 20.51 per cent while those who got jobs on account of special influence or acquaintence were 5.12 per cent of the total in service.

The data of the type and position of the service received by all the 39 persons are presented in Table 9.41. Here, we have 20.51 per cent of persons got jobs as peons. The same percentage of persons got jobs as technicians in textile industry. There were 15.38 per cent in the categories of clerk and teacher. In the same way, there were 7.69 per cent of persons who worked as sanitary workers or electric operators. It is interesting to note that there were only 2 persons *i.e.* 5.12 per cent who served as Talati-

TABLE 9.39: Persons in Service by Sex and Age

District	Sex and Age-groups																	
	6 - 14			15 - 29			30 - 44			45 - 59			60 & above			Total		
	M	F	Total	M	F	Total	M	F	Total	M	F	Total	M	F	Total	M	F	Total
Ahmedabad	-	-	-	4	-	4	2	-	2	1	-	1	-	-	-	7	-	7
Kaira	-	-	-	2	-	2	8	-	8	3	-	3	-	-	-	13	-	13
Mehsana	-	-	-	8	-	8	5	-	5	-	-	-	-	-	-	13	-	13
Surendranagar	1	-	1	3	-	3	1	-	1	1	-	1	-	-	-	6	-	6
Total	1	-	1	17	-	17	16	-	16	5	-	5	-	-	-	39	-	39

TABLE 9.40: Number of Persons and Channels of Getting Services

District	No.of persons in service	Of ones own efforts	Through employment exchange	Through special influence
Ahmedabad	7	6 (85.71)	1 (14.78)	-
Kaira	13	10 (76.92)	2 (15.38)	1 (7.69)
Mehsana	13	8 (61.53)	4 (30.76)	1 (7.69)
Surendranagar	6	5 (83.33)	1 (16.66)	-
Total	39 (100.00)	29 (74.35)	8 (20.51)	2 (5.12)

cum-Mantri in Village Panchayats. There was one person each who got jobs as Post Master, Social Worker and automobile driver.

In Table 9.42, we have data throwing light on whether the scheduled caste members doing service in different places experienced being treated as untouchables by their colleagues of high castes. It is interesting to note that 89.74 per cent of the members said that untouchability was not observed at the place of work. However, 10.25 per cent reported that untouchability was observed in the place of their work.

The number of individuals in scheduled caste households employed in miscellaneous services being less than 10, the data are presented now in descriptive form and not in tabulated form for economy of space. Out of 240 households, only 7 reported of having one person each in miscellaneous occupations. This means that 7 (2.92%) persons worked in miscellaneous occupations while 233 (97.08%) were not so engaged.

Again, out of 7 persons engagd in miscellaneous occupations, all were males, falling in the age group between 30 to 60 and above. However, it is significant to note that 4 persons out of 7 fell in the age group of 45 to 59.

The 7 households from where the same number of persons were in miscellaneous occupations received the total income of Rs. 8750 per annum. This means that the income of a household or person from this kind of jobs per annum was Rs. 1,250.

Regarding households sub-castes and their income from miscellaneous occupations, it was found that 3 persons from Vankar households were earning annually Rs. 3,300. There were 2 persons from Charmar households who annually earned Rs. 2,650. There was one person from Garoda household who was earning annually Rs. 2,300 from

TABLE 9.41: Number of Persons with Type and Position in Services

District	No.of persons in service	Peon	Artisan in textile mill	Clerk	Teacher	Sani-tation work	Electric operator	Talati-cum Mantri	Post master	Social work	Driver
Ahmedabad	7	1 (14.28)	3 (42.85)	1 (14.28)	-	-	1 (14.28)	-	1 (14.28)	-	-
Kaira	13	4 (30.76)	1 (7.69)	1 (7.69)	3 (30.07)	2 (15.38)	1 (7.69)	1 (7.69)	-	-	-
Mehsana	13	3 (23.07)	1 (7.69)	4 (30.76)	2 (15.38)	-	1 (7.69)	-	-	1 (7.69)	1 (7.69)
Surendranagar	6	-	3 (50.00)	-	1 (16.66)	1 (16.66)	-	1 (16.66)	-	-	-
Total	39 (100.00)	8 (20.51)	8 (20.51)	6 (15.38)	6 (15.38)	3 (7.69)	3 (7.69)	2 (5.12)	1 (2.56)	1 (2.56)	1 (2.56)

TABLE 9.42: Incidence of Observance of Untouchability at the Place of Service

District	No.of persons in service	No. one observes untouchability	Untouchability observing
Ahmedabad	7	7 (100.00)	-
Kaira	13	11 (84.61)	2 (15.38)
Mehsana	13	11 (84.61)	2 (15.38)
Surendranagar	6	6 (100.00)	-
Total	39 (100.00)	35 (89.74)	4 (10.25)

miscellaneous occupations. It is unique that income per person of Vankar and Chamar households was nearly half. One person from Valmik household earned only Rs. 500 per annum.

There was no household having any member engaged in miscellaneous occupations. There were two households who reported that 2 of their members respectively were engaged in miscellaneous occupations as principal activity and earned annually Rs. 3,000 in all. Those who reported that 5 of their members were occupied in miscellaneous occupations as subsidiary activity were 5 households.The annual income of these persons was Rs. 5,750 which amounted to Rs. 1,150 per annum per household. It is significant to note that this was much less than the income per household of those who were doing the miscellaneous services as principal activity.

It is significant to note that the average income of, household engaged in miscellaneous occupations in general was Rs. 1250 per annum.

As regards the income of households with members engaged in miscellaneous occupations, as only or principal activity, there were only 2 persons. They earned annually Rs. 3,000 as indicated before. However, the same number of households earned annually Rs. 1,420 from other occupations. It is significant to note that the average income per household with one person engaged in miscellaneous occupations as only or principal activity came to be Rs. 2,210.

Educated Unemployed

In Table 9.43, we find that there were 47 persons who reported that they

TABLE 9.43: Employment Position of Educated and Trained Persons

District	No.of unemployed persons	Educated or trained unemployed	Non-educated or untrained unemployed
Ahmedabad	15	-	15 (100.00)
Kaira	16	5 (31.25)	11 (68.75)
Mehsana	8	2 (25.00)	6 (75.00)
Surendranagar	8	-	8 (100.00)
Total	47 (100.00)	7 (14.89)	40 (85.10)

were unemployed. Out of these 14.89 per cent said that they were educated and trained but unemployed. The other group of unemployed were 85.10 per cent and all of them reported that they were not educated or trained for service.

In Table 9.44, we have data on employment seekers who had either registered themselves or had not done so for jobs through employment exchanges. There were 61.70 per cent out of 47 unemployed persons who said that they got their names registered with employment exchange. Those who said that they did not register their names in the employment exchange were 38.29 per cent .

TABLE 9.44: Employment Seekers Registered in Employment Exchange Bureau

District	No.of unemployed persons	Registered in employment exchange	Not registered in employment-exchange
Ahmedabad	15	12 (80.00)	3 (20.00)
Kaira	16	9 (56.25)	7 (43.75)
Mehsana	8	6 (75.00)	2 (25.00)
Surendranagar	8	2 (25.00)	6 (75.00)
Total	47	29 (61.70)	18 (38.29)

In Table 9.45, we have data throwing light on whether the unemployed persons were able to get interviews for jobs directly or otherwise. Here, we have 29.39 per cent of the candidates who said that they got interviews directly and 4.26 per cent said that they got interviews through employment exchange. Those who did not get interviews at all in spite of applications made by them were 65.95 per cent.

TABLE 9.45: Unemployed Persons Got and did not Get Interview Calls

District	No.of enemployed persons	Those who got interviews		Those who did not get Interviews
		Directly	Through employment exchange	
Ahmedabad	15	3 (20.00)	-	12 (80.00)
Kaira	16	5 (31.25)	1 (6.25)	10 (62.50)
Mehsana	8	5 (62.50)	1 (12.50)	2 (25.00)
Surendranagar	8	1 (12.50)	-	7 (87.50)
Total	47	14 (29.79)	2 (4.26)	31 (65.95)

In Table 9.46, we have data on whether the unemployed people who applied were successful or not in getting jobs. Out of 47 unemployed, 89.23 per cent said that they did not get jobs while 12.76 per cent said that they were successful in getting temporary employments.

TABLE 9.46: Success and Failure of Unemployed Persons in Getting Employment

District	No.of unemployed persons	Failures	Success in temporaries employment
Ahmedabad	15	12 (80.00)	3 (20.00)
Kaira	16	15 (93.75)	1 (6.25)
Mehsana	8	6 (75.00)	2 (25.00)
Surendranagar	8	8 (100.00)	-
Total	47	41 (87.23)	6 (12.76)

10

INCOME, INDEBTEDNESS, POVERTY AND ASSETS

Introduction

Although quite a sizeable data on occupations and income have already been presented in some of the earlier chapters, we present in this chapter the overall position of scheduled castes households under study. The picture that emerges gives an idea of the size and nature of earners and the level of income throwing light on the households living under poverty line.

We have also data on the extent of indebtedness of the sample households. It appears from the information presented in various tables, that SC people who used to depend heavily on private money lenders for borrowing money at high rate of interests, had begun to depend more on loans advanced at lower rate of interests by the Nationalised Banks, Government Agencies and the Co-operative Institutions.

One of the indicators of economic status of the scheduled castes can be to determine extent of household assets that they have in order to make their living conditions meaningful and comfortable. It is possible that assets of certain types can turn out to be liabilities to an individual or a household. However, this phenomenon is likely to vary and differ from case to case on the basis of different contexts in which an asset is interpreted as what it is. In brief, any addition to the household of a poor person is more or less likely to be an asset because out of nothing if something of utility in daily life comes in the family, it can be highly prestigious and stimulating to the members of the households. For a rich or affluent family who may be owning a car, a scooter, a fridge or a TV for instance, a situation may develop such that assets may become pieces of decoration and also liabilities in terms of expenditure and depreciation of value of goods. On the other hand, goods of minimum necessity are sources of contentment to a poor man.

Main Occupations and Earnings

To begin with, we try to know the classification of earners and non-earners among the scheduled castes according to sexes. Table 10.1 shows that the total number of members in 240 sample households were 1,478, of which 798 were males and 680 females. Out of these 51.49 per cent were earners while 48.51 per cent non-earners. Other details can be studied from the table itself.

In Table 10.2, we have data on the total number of 761 earning members, throwing light on the occupations from which they earned their income. The table shows that 3.02 per cent members were in the occupation of agriculture, 79.24 in agricultural labour, 5.12 per cent in service, 1.71 per cent in animal husbandry, 9.20 per cent in cottage industry, 0.79 per cent in trade and 0.92 per cent were in miscellaneous occupations.

The analysis of the reasons why 717 members of the sample households were non-earners as presented in Table 10.3. Out of 717 non-earners, 30.77 per cent males and 27.35 per cent females were children. The question of their becoming earning members immediately did not arise. Further, the young members of the scheduled castes households, who were studying, did not earn at all. This group consisted of 64.46 per cent males and 44.71 per cent females. There were 20.00 per cent of females who did not earn because of domestic responsibilities. There were 3.18 per cent of males and 7.06 per cent of females who said that they did not earn because of having reached the age of retirement. The number of those who reported their incapacity to earn due to sickness was negligible.

Levels of Income

Table 10.4 provides the classification of sample households according to occupations and sources of income. The total income of 240 households per annum was Rs. 11,95,217. Out of this, 88 households were in agriculture, earning 20.02 per cent of the total income of all the households of the sample. Those who derived income from agricultural labour were 204 households having 43.43 per cent of the total income per year. The number of households doing service was 35 and they derived 17.77 per cent of the total annual income. The households engaged in animal husbandry were in all 82 and they derived 8.69 per cent of the total income

TABLE 10.1 Earners and Non-earners by Sex

District	Total members			Earners			Non-earners		
	Males	Females	Total	Males	Females	Total	Males	Females	Total
Ahmedabad	215	171	386	120	79	199	95	92	187
Kaira	156	150	306	100	76	176	56	74	130
Mehsana	223	203	426	100	92	192	123	111	234
Surendranagar	204	156	360	101	93	194	103	63	166
Total	798	680	1478 (100.00)	421	340	761 (51.44)	377	340	717 (48.51)

TABLE 10.2 Earners Doing Major Occupations by Sex

District	Agriculture			Agricultural Labour			Service			Animal Husbandry			Cottage Industries			Trade			Any other			Total working members		
	M	F	Total	M	F	Total	M	F	Total	M	F	Total	M	F	Total	M	F	Total	M	F	Total	M	F	Total
Ahmedabad	4	1	5	96	70	166	7	—	7	1	2	3	9	6	15	1	—	1	2	—	2	120	79	199
Kaira	6	2	8	74	69	143	13	—	13	—	3	3	5	2	7	1	—	1	1	—	1	100	76	176
Mehsana	2	1	3	72	86	158	13	—	13	1	2	3	9	3	12	2	—	2	1	—	1	100	92	192
Surendrandagar	6	1	7	72	64	136	6	—	6	—	4	4	18	18	36	2	—	2	3	—	3	107	87	194
Total	18 (4.22)	5 (1.05)	23 (3.02)	314 (73.54)	289 (86.53)	603 (79.24)	39 (9.13)	—	39 (5.12)	2 (0.47)	11 (3.29)	13 (1.71)	41 (9.60)	29 (8.68)	70 (9.20)	6 (1.41)	—	6 (0.79)	7 (1.64)	—	7 (0.92)	427 (100.00)	334 (100.00)	761 (100.00)

TABLE 10.3 Non-earning Members by Sex

District	No. of non-earning Members			Due to Childhood		Taking Education		Domestic responsibility		Retirement		Sickness	
	Total	M	F	Male	Female	Male	Female	Male	Female	Male	Female	Male	Female
Ahmedabad	183	95	92	26	23	61	39	—	19	5	9	3	2
Kaira	130	56	74	13	12	42	38	—	17	1	06	—	1
Mehsana	234	123	111	43	30	75	45	—	29	2	7	3	—
Surendranager	166	103	63	34	28	65	30	—	3	4	2	—	—
Total	717	377 (100.00)	340 (100.00)	116 (30.77)	93 (27.35)	243 (64.46)	152 (44.71)	—	68 (20.00)	12 (3.18)	24 (7.06)	6 (1.59)	3 (0.88)

TABLE 10.4 The Main Sources of Income of Households

District	Agriculture		Agri. and other Labour		Service		Animal Husbandary		Cottage Industry		Trade		Other		Total	
	Main source of income of sample households															
	No. of H.H.	Income Rs.	No. of H.H.	Income Rs.	No. of H.H.	Income Rs.	No. of H.H.	Income Rs.	No. of H.H.	Income Rs.	No. of H.H.	Income Rs.	No. of H.H.	Income Rs.	No. of H.H.	Income Rs.
Ahmedabad	26	50,365	51	1,38,100	7	35200	15	17,698	10	11,300	1	1000	2	3700	60	2,57,363
Kaira	17	46,529	51	1,24,635	12	72890	15	22,060	5	24,575	1	5000	1	1200	60	2,86,889
Mehsana	21	66,161	55	1,42,065	10	75000	27	40,564	9	11,825	2	5200	1	2400	60	3,43,215
Surendranagar	24	76,412	47	1,14,290	6	29245	25	23,648	21	60,825	2	1700	3	1450	60	3,07,750
Total	88	2,39,467 (20.02)	204	5,19,090 (43.43)	35	212,515 (17.77)	82	1,03,970 (8.69)	45	98,525 (8.24)	6	12900 (1.08)	7	8750 (0.73)	240 *	1195,217 (100.00)

The total do not tally due to overlapping categories.

per annum. The number of households engaged in cottage industry were 45 and they earned 8.24 per cent of the total income. The households working in trade and miscellaneous occupations were in all 6 and 7 respectively. It may be noted that the households practising trade had relatively better income than those engaged in miscellneous occuaptions.

In Table 10.5, we have data on the total income of sample households in terms of annual, monthly and daily income per household. The average income of the 240 households per annum was Rs. 4,984 and the monthly average was Rs. 415. The income per day of the sample households having an averge size of 6.16 members was Rs. 14 only.

TABLE 10.5 Overall Income of Households in Districts

District	Sample House-holds	Total annual income Rs.	Average income per annum Rs.	Average income per month Rs.	Average income per day Rs	Avr. size of H.H. Rs.
Ahmedabad	60	2,57,363	4,289	357	12	6.43
Kaira	60	2,86,889	4,781	398	13	5.00
Mehsana	60	3,43,215	5,720	476	16	7.00
Surendranagar	60	3,07,750	5,129	427	14	6.00
Total	240	11,95,217	4,980	415	14	6.16

In table 10.6 we have data throwing light on the annual, monthly and daily income of households of sub-castes of scheduled castes. The number of Vankar households in the sample were 117 whose average annual income per household was Rs. 5,488.04. The average income of this group of households per month was Rs. 457.34 and per day, it was Rs. 15.24. The number of households of the Chamar were 71 and their average household income per annum was Rs. 4,881.80, per month Rs. 406.75 and per day Rs. 33.83. The number of Valmik households were 33 whose average income per annum was Rs. 3,807.79, monthly income Rs. 371.25 and daily income Rs. 26.43. There were 9 Garoda households on the sample whose average annual income was Rs. 5,668.44, monthly income Rs. 472.33 and daily Rs. 15.78. There were Senva households whose annual average income was Rs. 3,089.38 and monthly income Rs. 257.42, while daily income was Rs. 8.57. The remaining 2 households form other sub-castes. Their average annual income was Rs. 3,060.00, monthly income Rs. 255 and daily income was Rs. 8.50. It is significant to note that the average income of households of Garoda, Chamar and Valmiki sub-casts came to be very much above the overall average of Rs. 13.83 per day.

The average income of Vanker sub-caste per day was slightly higher than the average income of the whole group. But the daily income of Senva, Barot, Turi and others was very much below the average daily income of the sub-castes in general.

TABLE 10.6 Income of Households of Sub-castes

Main-Sub-castes	No. of sample House-holds	Total income of the Group	Average H.H. income per annum	Average H.H. income per month	Average H.H. income per day	Average size of H.H.
Vankar	117	6,41,261	5488.04	457.34	15.24	6.37
Chamar	71	3,46,448	4881.80	406.75	33.83	3.37
Valmik	33	1,25,657	3807.79	317.25	26.42	5.18
Garoda	9	51,016	5668.44	472.33	15.74	5.78
Senva	8	24,715	3089.38	257.42	8.57	6.00
Barot/Turi & others	2	6,120	3060.00	255.00	8.50	5.00
Total	240	11,95,217	4984.24	415.33	13.83	6.16

In Table 10.7, we have district wise data on the income of scheduled castes sub-castes. Here, we find that 48.75 per cent of Vankar had 53.68 per cent income of the total income of 240 households. The Chamar households were 29.58 of the total and they shared 28.98 of the total income per annum. The Valmiki were 13.75 per cent sharing 10.50 per cent of the total income. The households of Garoda made 3.75 per cent of the total sample households and earned 4.26 per cent of the total income. The Senva households were 3.33 per cent, earning 2.07 per cent of the total income and the others made 0.83 per cent of households erning 0.51 per cent of the total income of sample households.

In Table 10.8, we have data on number of households falling in different annual income brackets. There were 14 households in the income bracket of 0 to 1,500 per annum. This indeed was a very pathetic situation for the households who were very much below the poverty line. The next income bracket of Rs. 1,500 to Rs. 3,500 includes 76 households. They were no doubt slightly better in terms of annual income than the most poor set of households. However, they were also below the poverty line. The number of households who fell in the income bracket of Rs. 350 to Rs. 5000 were 62. Those in the bracket of Rs. 5,001 to Rs. 10,000 were 70. This means that the largely number of 70 sample households were just above the poverty line. The number of rich households in the income bracket of Rs. 10,001 to 15,000 were 13. While very rich households above the

TABLE 10.7 : Income of Sub-caste Households in Districts

District	Vankar		Chamar		Bhangi		Garoda		Senva & others		Barot-Turi		Total	
	No. of H.H.	Rs.	No. of H.H.	Rs.	No. of H.H.	Rs.	No. of H.H.	Rs.	No. of H.H.	Rs.	No. of H.H.	Rs.	No. of H.H.	Rs.
Ahmedabad	33	1,60,644	17	62,624	2	7,810	3	9,370	3	10,795	2	6,120	60	2,57,863
Kaira	20	1,00,873	21	95,623	14	55,363	5	35,030	-	—	—	—	60	2,86,889
Mehsana	24	1,64,860	25	1,47,925	6	16,510	—	—	5	13,920	—	—	60	3,43,215
Surendranagar	40	2,14,884	8	40,276	11	45,974	1	6,616	—	—	—	—	60	3,07,750
Total	117 (48.75)	6,41,261 (53.68)	71 (29.58)	3,46,448 (28.98)	33 (13.75)	1,25,657 (10.50)	9 (3.75)	51,016 (4.26)	8 (3.33)	24,715 (2.07)	2 (0.83)	6,120 (0.51)	240 (100.00)	11,96,217 (100.00)

TABLE 10.8: Households Covered by Income Brackets Per Annum

Income brackets in Rs.	Ahmedabad		Kaira		Mehsana		Surendranager		Total	
	No. of HH	Total income Rs. p.a.	No. of H.H.	Total income Rs. p.a.	No. H.H.	Total income Rs. p.a.	No. of H.H.	Total income Rs. p.a.	No. of H.H.	Total income Rs. p.a.
0 - 1500	3	3560	5	6735	3	3590	3	3680	14	17560
1501- 3500	22	59261	20	49060	20	49351	14	37379	76	195051
3501- 5000	20	85014	16	69603	12	46970	14	58113	62	259700
5001- 10000	13	89998	13	85500	17	126989	27	173293	70	474780
10001- 15000	2	20530	5	59711	5	62215	1	10231	13	152687
More than 15000	-	-	1	26280	3	54100	1	25054	5	95434
Total	60	257363	60	286889	60	343215	60	307750	240	1195217

bracket of Rs. 15,000 and above per annum were only 5. This means that out of 240 sample households, 88 or 33.66 per cent H.H. were above poverty line.

Extent of Indebtedness

Berore Independence, the scheduled castes in need of emergency had no alternative but to go to a private moneylender. The situation has some what changed in this respect because of special privileges and asistance offered to them by the financing institutions in the public sector.

We find from Table 10.9 that out of 240 sample households there were 44.58 per cent of households who had taken loan either for agriculture or for social purpose. There were 55.41 per cent of the households who had not taken loans from any source. It is likely that these people when in need of money might be taking recourse to borrowing money from close relations for short period of time.

TABLE 10.9 Households Who had Taken Loans

District	No. of H.H.	Loan taking H.H.	H.H. having not taken loan
Ahmedabad	60	37 (61.66)	23 (38.33)
Kaira	60	29 (48.33)	31 (51.66)
Mehsana	60	22 (36.66)	38 (63.33)
Surendranagar	60	19 (31.66)	41 (68.33)
Total	240	107 (44.58)	133 (55.41)

Table 10.10 presents data on the sources from where loans were taken by 107 households. 19.62 per cent households said that they took loans from cooperative institutions and 28.03 per cent households had taken loan from government agencies and institutions. It is significant to note that 88.78 per cent of the households reported that they took loan from private individuals. it is natural that the totals do not tally because of overlapping catagories.

Table 10.11 gives a comparative picture of the amount of loans taken by households from various loan giving sectors, so to say. The total amount of loan taken by the households concerned from cooperative sector was

TABLE 10.10 : Sources from where Loans were Taken

District	No. of H.H. taking loan	Loan by H.H. from Co-operative institutions	Loans by H.H. from Govt. agencies	Loans by H.H. from private individual
Ahmedabad	37	7	9	35
		(18.91)	(24.32)	(94.59)
Karia	29	1	33	25
		(3.44)	(37.93)	(86.20)
Meshana	22	3	5	22
		(13.63)	(22.72)	(100)
Surendranagar	19	10	5	13
		(52.63)	(26.32)	(68.42)
Total	107	21	30	95
	(100)	(19.62)	(28.03)	(88.78)

*Total do not tally due to overlapping categories

Rs. 30,400 which amounted to Rs. 284 per household. The amount of loan taken from public sector organisations was Rs. 52,650 which amounts to Rs. 492 per household. Those who took loans form private sector, received the total of Rs. 1,76,250. The average loan per household in this sector came to be Rs. 1,647. This shows that scheduled castes households prefered private moneylender for loans on considerably high rate of interest and some of them may not be registered money lenders.

In Table 10.12, we have presented data on number of houeholds with or without membership of cooperative institutions helpful to scheduled castes in advancing loans at lower rate of interest. Here, we find that out of 240 sample households, there were 22.91 per cent who were members of the cooperative societies. The remaining 77.08 per cent were not members of this institution.

We shall now find out from Table 10.13 as to how many of those who were members of the cooperative society received loan. Out of 55 such households, 38.18 per cent had taken loans from cooperative institutions, while 61.82 per cent had not taken loans from cooperative institutions.

Table 10.14 presents data on the number of households and the amount of loan taken from various cooperative institutions by 21 households. It is interesting to note that all the 21 households had taken loans from only Service Cooperative Societies to the tune of Rs. 30,400, and it came to be the average loan of Rs. 1,448 per household. None of the households had taken loan from Land Mortgage Bank or Urban Cooperative Bank.

In Table 10.15, we have information on households who took loans

TABLE 10.11 Loans Taken by Households from Different Sources

District	No.of H.H.	Co.operative Sector		Public Sector		Private Sector		Total	
		Amount of loan Rs	Average per H.H. Rs	Amount of loan Rs	Average per H.H. Rs	Amount of loan Rs	Average per H.H. Rs	Amount of loan Rs	Average per H.H. Rs
Ahmedabad	37	9600	259	10400	281	75950	2053	95950	2593
Kaira	29	800	28	26500	914	22300	769	49600	1710
Mehsana	22	6900	314	9450	430	50400	2290	66750	3034
Surendranagar	19	13100	689	6300	490	27600	1453	47000	2474
Total	107	30400	284	52650	492	176250	1647	259300	2423

TABLE 10.12 Households Having Membership of Co-operative Organisations

District	No.of H.H.	H.H.being members of co-operative institutions	H.H.being non-members
Ahmedabad	60	21 (35.00)	39 (65.00)
Kaira	60	11 (18.33)	49 (81.66)
Mehsana	60	9 (15.00)	51 (85.00)
Surendranagar	60	14 (23.33)	46 (76.66)
Total	240	55 (22.91)	185 (77.08)

TABLE 10.13 Households Taking Loans from Co-operative Organisations

District	No.of member	No.of loan loan taking H.H.	No.of H.H. not taking loan
Ahmedabad	21	7 (33.33)	14 (66.66)
Kaira	11	1 (9.09)	10 (90.90)
Mehsana	9	2 (22.22)	7 (77.77)
Surendranagar	14	10 (71.42)	4 (28.57)
Total	55	20 (36.36)	35 (63.63)

from statutory financial institutions operating in public sector. There were in all 30 households who took loans from public sector institutions and their total borrowings were Rs. 52,650 which came to be Rs. 1,755 per household. Those who took loans from Nationalised Banks were 23 and the total amount of loan taken was Rs. 42,850 which for an average household was Rs. 1,863. This was the highest amount of loan taken by the scheduled castes households from public sector institutions. It is significant to note that only 2 households got total loans of Rs. 2,000 from Scheduled Castes Development Corporation of the State Government. Those who received Takavi loans or subsidy were in all 5 households and the total amount came to be Rs. 6,800 and per household it was Rs. 1,700.

In Table 10.16, we have presented data throwing light on the number

TABLE 10.14 Loans Taken from Service Co-operative Societies

(Co-operative Sector)

District	Service Co-operative Society			Total		
	No.of H.H.	Total loan Rs.	Average loan per H.H. Rs.	No.of H.H.	Total loan Rs.	Average loan per Rs.
Ahmedabad	7 (11.67)	9600	1371	7 (11.67)	9600	1371
Kaira	1 (1.67)	800	800	1 (1.67)	800	800
Mehsana	3 (5.00)	6900	2300	3 (5.00)	6900	2300
Surendranagar	10 (16.67)	13100	1310	10 (16.67)	13100	1310
Total	21 (8.75)	30400	1448	21 (8.75)	30400	1448

of households who took loan from private sector. In all, there were 95 households who took Rs. 1,76,250 as loan from private individuals. This means that the indebtedness of scheduled castes from private sector was Rs. 1,855 per household. There were 40 households who took loans from moneylenders and the average loan came to be Rs. 3,036. Those who had taken loans from business houses were 31 and the average loan per household was Rs. 1,018. Those who took loans from relatives and friends were 24 households and their average indebtedness in this intimate circle of relationship was Rs. 969 only.

Assessment of Household Assets

We have indicated earlier that additions of assets to poor households such as those of scheduled castes and backward classes are useful and welcome. The assets can be movable as well as immovable property.

In this section especially, we talk of assessment of movable property in the possession of the sample households. Except one table throwing light on the type and value of houses in which these people live, the data on other assets are presented without reproducing tables due to scanty figures.

In Table 10.17, we have data throwing light on the number of scheduled castes households with kutcha or pucca houses and the total value of the same. Out of 240 households, there are 197 or 82.08 per cent

TABLE 10.15 Loans Taken from Public Institution (Public Sector)

District	Nationalised Banks			Scheduled Castes Development Corporation			Govt. Takavi Loan or subsidy			Total		
	No.of H.H.	Amount of loan Rs.	Average per HH Rs.	No.of H.H	Amount of loan Rs.	Average per HH Rs.	No.of H.H.	Amt.of loan Rs.	Average perHH Rs.	No.of H.H.	Amt. of loan Rs.	Average per HH Rs.
Ahmedabad	5 (8.33)	4400	880	2 (3.33)	3000	1500	2 (3.33)	3000	1500	9 (15.00)	10400	1156
Kaira	11 (18.33)	26500	2406	—	—	—	—	—	—	11 (18.33)	26500	2409
Mehsana	5 (8.33)	9450	1890	—	—	—	—	—	—	5 (8.33)	9450	1890
Surendranagar	2 (3.33)	2500	1250	—	—	—	3 (5.00)	3800	1267	5 (8.33)	6300	1250
Total	23 (9.58)	42850	1863	2 (0.83)	3000	1500	5 (2.08)	6800	1360	30 (12.50)	52650	1755

TABLE 10.16 Loans Taken from Private Parties (Private sector)

District	Money-lenders			Business houses			Relatives and Friends			Total		
	No. of H.H.	Amount of loan Rs.	Average per H.H. Rs.	No. of H.H.	Amount of loan Rs.	Average per HH Rs.	No. of H.H.	Amount of loan Rs.	Average per H.H. Rs.	No.of H.H.	Amount of loan Rs.	Average per H.H. Rs.
Ahmedabad	15 (25.00)	54550	3637	7 (2.92)	8600	1229	13 (21.67)	12800	985	35 (58.33)	75950	2170
Kaira	6 (10.00)	12500	2083	13 (21.67)	6850	527	6 (10.00)	2950	492	25 (41.67)	22300	892
Mehsana	12 (20.00)	38900	3242	8 (13.37)	8500	1062	2 (3.33)	3000	1500	22 (36.67)	50400	2291
Surendranagar	7 (11.67)	15500	2214	3 (1.25)	7600	2533	3 (5.00)	4500	1500	13 (21.67)	27600	2123
Total	40 (16.67)	121450	3036	31 (12.92)	31550	1018	24 (10.00)	23250	969	95 (39.58)	176250	1855

TABLE 10.17 Type of Houses Owned as Assets by Households

District	No.of H.H.	Katcha House		Pacca House		Thatch Roof hut	
		No.of H.H.	Value Rs.	No.of H.H.	Value Rs.	No.of H.H	Value Rs.
Ahmedabad	60	42 (70.00)	228500	16 (26.67)	131200	2 (3.33)	5000
Kaira	60	52 (86.66)	250750	4 (6.67)	46300	4 (6.67)	7000
Mehsana	60	57 (95.00)	353800	3 (5.00)	35000	—	—
Surendranagar	60	46 (76.67)	257000	11 (18.33)	117000	3 (5.00)	4000
Total	240	197 (82.08)	1090050	34 (14.17)	329500	9 (3.75)	16000

with Kutcha houses. The value assessment of this immovable property of the households came to be Rs. 10,90,050. The number of households having pucca houses were only 14.17 per cent, and the total value of the property came to be Rs. 3,29,500.

The assorted data of other assets are scanty and variable from item to item. Therefore, we present salient aspects of the same in the following lines without presenting the tables concerned. Out of 240 households, 33 (13.75%) had miscellaneous tools useful in agriculture. The total value of these assets came to be Rs. 2,04,597.

The number of households with bullock carts of their own were 14 (23.33%) and the total value was Rs. 29,700. The number of households with field wells for irrigation were 7 of the value of Rs. 80,500. The number of households with facility of pumping machine sets was only 5 and the value of this was Rs. 25,000. There was one household with a tube well worth Rs. 40,000, another with a hand-pump for water worth Rs. 1,500. Besides, one household had the facility of spraying equipment for insecticides, worth Rs. 500.

The items of furniture, personal conveniences, storage, entertainment and personal transport were as follows. Out of 240 households, there were 230 who had cots, the value of which came to be Rs. 49,150. There were 66 households with wooden chests worth Rs. 4,605. In all, 53 households had bicycles of their own the value of which came to be Rs. 14,700. There was no household with motor cycle, scooter or motor car. There were 39 households with radio sets worth Rs. 11,700. Those who had tables and chairs as items of furniture were 39 and the total value of these assets was Rs. 4,625. There was no household with a sofa set.

There were 32 households who said that they had the facility of suit cases and boxes for storing personal cloths, valuable linnens, etc., the value of which came to be Rs. 1,485. Those who said that they had single beds for sleeping comforts came to be only 12 and the value of the same was reported to be Rs. 980. There were 11 households with the facility of cupboards whose value came to be Rs. 3,090. There were only 2 households having table fans and ceiling fans worth Rs. 1,500.

It is significant to note that the total value of all the assets reported in earlier items found with all the 240 households came to be Rs. 91,385. This means that the average value of assets of the scheduled castes households came to be Rs. 381.

There were 166 households who had displayed decorative wall hangings in the form of pictures and photographs. The total value of such pieces was Rs. 3,489. Those who were in possession of idols for worship were 57 households and the value of the same came to be Rs. 693. There were only 3 households with musical instruments which go with singing of prayer, folk-songs, etc. worth Rs. 150. The total value of a variety of these assets was Rs. 4,361 which came to be Rs. 18 per household.

The value of personal attires and cloths for daily wear for the members of the households came to be Rs. 1,23,525. The mattress for retiring at night, day-time rest and instant sickness for the members of 234 households was reported to value in all Rs. 50,480. There were 126 households in possession of quilts, bed sheets, etc., the total value of which came to be Rs. 9,050. The number of households in possession of pillows were 128 worth Rs. 3,857.

The facilities of wearing shoes and slippers were with 219 households and the total value of which came to be Rs. 10,340. There were 129 households who reported to be in possession of fountain pens worth Rs. 1,163. The number of households who reported to be in possession of books, magazines and other book-lets reading materials of religious or secular nature, etc., were 61. The worth of these assets for awareness, knowledge and entertainment came to be in all worth Rs. 5,495. The overall picture shows that the total value of this group of household assets with the sample households was Rs. 2,03,910. The average value of such asset per household came to be Rs. 850.

With respect to ornaments of gold and silver as well as weapons of defence and offence in possession of the sample households, it was found that 48 households were in possession of these worth Rs. 92,185. Besides, there were 53 households with silver ornaments, the total value of which came to be Rs. 1,00,650. There were 2 households with ornaments of semi-precious metal worth Rs. 325. No household reported having deadly weapons of offence and defence.

With respect to items of domestic necessity, kitchen ware gagets, etc., all the 240 households reported that they were in possession of eating plates, mugs, pots and dishes useful in serving food and drinks. The total value of the same came to be Rs. 31,640. The households with cups, bowls etc., of metal, China ware, glass, etc., were 239. The value of these came to be Rs. 12,282. Those who were in possession of cooking vassels e.g. cans, pans, etc., were 236 households. The total value of these assets was reported to be Rs. 23,201. Besides, miscellaneous kitchen wares in possession of 224 households was reported to be of the value of Rs. 14,512. There were only 207 households who reported to be in possession of water vessels, containers and pitchers. The total value of these assets was reported to be Rs. 24,650. The smaller items for drinking purpose such as tea cups, tumblers, etc., were reported to be in possession of 194 households, the value of which was Rs. 12,316.

The households in possession of water carriers such as buckets were 186, the total value of which came to be Rs. 7,572. The households in possession of large metal vessels such as trough for preparing food etc. were 168 and the total value of the same was reported to be Rs. 7,460.

There were only 70 households who were in possession of cooking primus stove costing in all Rs. 4,215. There were 58 households who reported that they had traditionl cooking stoves which can be operated with coal, wood, etc. The total value of these assets was reported to be Rs. 1,025. The overall picture indicates that the 240 households were in possession of a variety of such assets worth Rs. 1,38,873. This means that the average value of these assets per household was Rs. 579 only.

11

REVIEW OF LAND REFORMS AND DEVELOPMENT SCHEMES

Introduction

The main schedule prepared for interviewing the heads of individual households in this study included items of information helpful in reviewing the programme of land reforms to benefit the poor landless labourers of scheduled castes. There were also items that could throw light on the benefits received by the respondents through the implementation of different schemes for all round development of scheduled castes. Pointed questions were asked as to whether the respondents were aware of provisions of various types of schemes for their benefit through various programmes of the government including special 20-Point Programme. Point No. 7 in this progamme is exclusively geared to accelerate implementation of developmental programme for scheduled castes and scheduled tribes. We tried to find out also whether the respondents were aware of the special Component Plan Schemes and Scheduled Castes Economic Development Corporation of the State Government.

Now we shall concentrate our attention on the important aspects of land reforms and the schemes envisaged for development of scheduled castes. To begin with, we shall review the actual state of land reforms from which members of scheduled castes might have benefited. Later on we shall summarise general findings of the extent of benefits derived by scheduled castes on the basis of empirical data analysed and discussed in the previous chapters. In the end, we shall present statistical information based on the interviews of the households on their awareness and knowledge of the efforts made by the government and welfare agencies providing specific assistance for the development of scheduled castes.

Review of Land Reforms

Since the programme of land reforms is meant to benefit all categories of depressed classes of people including scheduled castes, and tribes, and backward classes, the analysis presented here will have certain common features applicable to all such groups also.

The programme for giving land for cultivation to the households of the depressed classes whether they are owner cultivators or agricultural labourers, was envisaged by the government in implementing the following two legal items of land reforms:

(1) Gujarat Agricultural Land Ceiling Act.
(2) Bombay Tenancy Legislation.

In the first instance, it should be noted that the Land Ceiling Act was implemented in the state of Gujarat on 1.9.1961. Amendments were made in this act from time to time as required. Under this Act, the surplus land in possession of any landholders which was more than the ceiling prescribed by the act was to be returned to the government. The land recovered by the government in this manner was to be given to the members of scheduled castes and scheduled tribes. An amendment was introduced in this act by the Gujarat Government on 1.4.1976 whereby the definition of the household who can get benefits from this Act was revised.

(a) The revised definition of a household eligible for receiving land under Land Ceiling Act was indeed a revolutionary step taken by the State Government. According to this definition, every adult male member was to be identified as an independent unit eligible for right over land for self-cultivation. This means that when the ceiling act came into force, all the adult sons of the landholder became eligible for getting one unit of land from the total land of the father.

In cases where a household had land, disproportionately larger than the needs of adult sons, the surplus land had to be given to the government. The government could have got a lot of surplus land under this act. However, when the programme was implemented on the ground, many irregularities were committed by the landholders under the connivance of the government machinery. This nullified the scope of the government receiving enough surplus land for helping the landless households of scheduled castes and scheduled tribes. In fact, what happened after the introduction of new definition of a household eligible for possession of land was that the government received only 1/10th of the total surplus land which otherwise could have been received on the basis of land ceiling act.

It appears that the government machinery which has been created for implementing the land ceiling act for the benefit of the weaker sections of the society has proved to be counter productive. According to the opinion of a layman in the village society, had the government spent the money required for administrative expenditure under this act, only for buying new land from the open market for distribution among the households of the target group, it could have been more useful to landless persons and economical to the government exchequer.

The government was, however, able to recover 18,598 hectares of land as surplus under land ceiling act before the introduction of the new definition of eligibility from 1.4.1976 for the share of a son in the land of the father. Out of this, the government was in possession of 18,005 hectares of land of which 17,766 hectares of land had been distributed among the members of scheduled castes and scheduled tribes. The number of scheduled castes members who received land under this programme was 9,937 and the total land distributed among them was 7,777 hectares. In the same way, 1,497 members of the scheduled tribes were given 2,453 hectares of land under this scheme. The remaining 7,536 hectares of land was distributed among 3,307 persons of other backward classes.

(b) After the introduction of new land regulation of 1-4-1976 with regard to the partition of land through inheritance, the Government of Gujarat had declared 66,975 hectares of land as surplus for distribution among the weaker sections of the society. The Government had in reality taken possession of only 31,500 hectares of land out of which it was possible to distribute 14,232 hectares of land among weaker sections for good. Moreover, it was possible for the government to distribute 5,577 hectares of land on year to year basis upto 31-8-1983.

1. Of the land distributed for good, the 804 scheduled tribes people got 1,584 hectares of land . The number of persons of scheduled castes who were distributed land during this period was 3,601, and in all they got 8,416 hectares of surplus land. The remaining surplus land had been distributed among the members of other backward communities. There were, however, cases pending in the court of law with regard to 22,535 hectares of land to be

released for possession of the government under the Land Ceiling Act.

2. Under the Bombay Tenancy Legislation Act, a person who is actually tilling the land was given the ownership of the land. The persons of scheduled castes and scheduled tribes who were earlier cultivating the land as tenants had all become the owners of and after filing claim suits in the court of law. Under this Act, 77,552 tenants from scheduled castes and scheduled tribes became owners of 1,81,162 hectares of land. The remaining 3,73,053 hectares of land was distributed with ownership right to 1,78,644 persons of other backward communities.

This act no doubt gave the impression of being helpful to these people. However, the amount of land distributed to individuals came to be so small that it became difficult for a person to maintain his family from the income derived from the produce of the land. This was more so because many of them had to mortgage their land on account of money borrowed during social ceremonies, sickness, etc. The small area of land received by an individual under the tenancy legislation is not alienable by law and, therefore, it was not possible for the person to sell it to anybody. There were many cases, however, where such land was virtually in the possession of the moneylenders or better off land owners who were enjoying the produce of the land.

The Government had distributed also other types of waste land to scheduled castes and scheduled tribes in rural areas. This kind of land is not alienable as per the conditions laid down by the government. Unfortunately, because of indebtedness of these people such land was also virtually sold in concealed form to the money lenders. The only evidence that it was in the name of the owner was that the underhand transfer of land had not been put on the government records. This was a great dilemma for the people and the government interested in introducing land reforms for the betterment of all categories of backward classes.

About 2 to 3 acres of land, which was generally the quota fixed for distribution, is not sufficient for a person to invest in equipments and other necessary facilities for improved cultivation. This is another reason why the poor family was not able to use sufficiently the schemes of improved seeds, fertilizers, insecticides, irrigation facilities, etc. The result of all these difficulties and handicaps, was that the recepient of land looked upon possession of land as a liability rather than an asset. In the long run he transfers land to another person under illegal mortgage or sale deed, and subverts the purpose of land reforms.

The above situation needs to be remedied if the government wants that land reforms become really benefitial to the members of the scheduled castes and scheduled tribes to whom land is distributed for self-cultivation. It seems that the following measures, if adopted by the government, may become helpful in the long run to provide self-sufficiency to the scheduled castes and scheduled tribes in holding land for self-cultivation.

(1) The plot of land to be given to an individual under the land reforms act should be of such a size that it is possible for the households to depend entirely on its income for livelihood. The size of such plot may vary from place to place on account of local conditions and quality of soil.

(2) It is also necessary that the beneficiaries of land reforms are provided with full economic assitance to buy land through scheduled banks without interest. For, once scheduled castes or scheduled tribes households become self-sufficient through land for cultivation, they will not presumably approach the government often. Wherever, a plot of land is not available to make a household self-sufficient through land for cultivation, such people be provided jobs in industrial sector and helped in developing cottage industries whose products can be easily sold in the market.

The Government of India organised a seminar on Employment of Scheduled Castes and Scheduled Tribes some time in 1964. The Members of Parliament, officers of Ministry of Home Affairs, Planning Commission and others participated in the Seminar. The report was published by the Government of India Press in 1965. The problem of employment of these people was related to the problem of education in the sense that these people could not be employed if they were not properly qualified for the jobs reserved for them.

The participants thought it was wise to discuss the problem of land as an alternative means of employment for these people. One can find enlightening recommendations on availability of land for distribution to these people on page 39 of the Seminar Report. It says "Enforcement of land reforms particularly in regard to ceilings, specifically the present tendencey to have the ceiling of 30 standard acres or so, severely restricted the scope of this measure as a tool for the amelioration of employment problem in agriculture. A much lower ceiling world have to be fixed depending on the proportion of landless labourers in the particular state".

The land mark in the efforts towards the development for scheduled castes has been the establishment of the Working Group on Development of Scheduled Castes, 1980-85. The first meeting of the Working Group was convened by the Ministry of Home Affairs, New Delhi in 1981. The report has been presented by the Working Group giving targets and recommendations on a number of subjects directly concerned with all round development of scheduled castes. It deals with the benefits likely to flow from the outlays of previous plans.

Since we are concerned mainly with the land for cultivation and house sites in this reports, we take note of some of the measures recommended by the Working Group summarised in the following points:—

1. In order to improve the economic conditions of scheduled castes in rural areas, we have to take care of measures for expansion of land resources for the people of this community.
2. The ceiling law on land be so implemented that it becomes helpful in the distribution of land peacefully to the secheduled castes on priority basis.
3. Land owned by the Central or State Government or any other Public Authority or Institution, not required for any public purpose and Bhoodan and Gramdan Lands be distributed among the landless poor agricultural labourers with due priority for scheduled castes.
4. Land belonging to Central and State Government or Public Institutions, which cannot be permanently distributed to any private individual on account of reservation for public purpose, be let out on lease and licence for as long term as possbile to landless poor people with due priority for scheduled castes. Care be taken to see that complete package of all necessary assistance such as irrigation facilities, bullocks, agricultural implements, inputs etc. are also provided to them through loan or subsidy.
5. Land records be brought upto date by including all names of members of the scheduled castes who have been given land by the Government. Also, it includes necessity of keepig up-to-date land records of land received by them from other sources.
6. Since a large number of scheduled castes are working as landless agricultural labourers, the Special Component Plan of the states, and also Plans of the Ministry of Agriculture and Rural Reconstruction must earmark and channalise adequate share of finances for scheduled castes.

It is needless to say that the recommendations of the Working Group are loudable as can be seen from just a few instrumentalities high lighted below for speedy development of scheduled castes. They are:

(1) Special Component Plans of the State as well as Central Ministry.
(2) Special Central Assistance for the Special Component Plans of the State and Centre, and
(3) Scheduled Castes Development Corporations in the States.

Review of Development Schemes

It was revealed from the present survey that a large section of the scheduled castes in rural areas depended generally on the occupation of agricultural labour. They were exploited lot in many respects. The government, therefore, provided a number of schemes for their development under the Special Component Plan. The resources of the Special Component Plan for the scheduled castes came from the (i) Scheduled Castes Economic Development Corporation, (ii) Scheduled Banks, and (iii) Centrally Sponsored Economic Assistance.

It is interesting to note from the documents of the Government of Gujarat on Special Component Plan for Scheduled Castes 1983-84 that the first SCP was initially started with an outlay of Rs. 9.06 crores for 1979-80. However, the total expenditure incurred by the government during this period was Rs. 5.06 crores. The provision in the SCP during the subsequent years was increased. The flow of Central Assistance was estimated at Rs. 3.00 crores. According to the plan worked out for helping 50.00 percent of the scheduled castes households, about 5,000 to 55,000 households were to be helped to cross the poverty line every year during the Sixth 5 year plan. The outlay and the expenditure declared by the government during the 5 years of the 6th plan is presented below.

(Rs. in lacs)

Year	Outlays	Expenditure
1979-80	906.21	506.43
1980-81	2387.74	1351.93
1981-82	2478.89	1751.90
1982-83	2651.67	1075.77 (upto Dec. 82)
1983-84	2731.00	2731.00 (anticipated)

Special Component Plan and the Outlays for 1983-84

The data presented in this section has been derived from the Government document on SCP for 1983-84, referred to earlier. The main purpose of giving actual figures of outlays proposed for expenditure on various schemes for the development of scheduled castes is to provide a general profile of economic assistance to be used for implementing different schemes. It does not mean, however, that the benefits of different schemes have reached the scheduled castes households at the ground level. We shall now take up the presentation of SCP outlays proposed by various schemes.

In the 1983-84 annual plan of the State Government, Rs. 55.00 lacs were earmarked for crop husbandry. With regard to land reforms, government provided an outlay of Rs. 12.00 lacs, for minor irrigation Rs. 53.00 lacs, soil conservation Rs. 22.00 lacs, animal husbandry Rs. 11.00 lacs, and forestry Rs. 6.00 lacs. There were other continuing programmes for which sufficient amount of money was provided under the schemes of NREP, SFDA, SFAL, DPAP, IRD, Antyodaya and Abhinav Gram Nirman. The schemes for local development workers, off season employment, block level planning, cooperation, power development, village and small industries, roads and bridges, general education, housing and social inputs were also provided for during 1983-84 from SCP outlays. There were other items on which provision had been made in order that the total upliftment of the scheduled castes was achieved as desired in the 20 Point Programme. The grand total of the expenditure for all these schemes proposed during 1983-84 under scheduled castes outlays were Rs. 2,731.00 lacs.

The Government of Gujarat took up a phased programme for the development of 1,411 villages with high concentration of scheduled castes population in the State. In the first year of the 6th Five year plan, 282 villages were identified and a house to house survey of the scheduled castes households was undertaken to assess their needs. During 1981-82, 316 more villages were identified. By the end of the 6th 5 year plan, 50.00 per cent of the scheduled castes households were to be covered. However, in the first two years of 1980-82, the total number of 45,000 households were assisted each year through the family oriented programme. During 1982-83 as many as 87,522 scheduled castes households were assisted.

A high power committee under the Chairmanship of the Chief Minister has been set up for reviewing the progress of Special Component Plan Programme. The district level committee under the Chairmanship of the Collector takes care of reviewing actual implementation of the programme.

Role of Gujarat Scheduled Castes Economic Development Corporation (GSCEDC)

This corporation was set up in 1979 in order to provide financial assistance for income generating programmes such as milch cattle, leather industry, weaving, tailoring, bullock and camal carts, village and cottage industries, etc.

A household with the income of Rs. 3,500 per annum was considered eligible for economic assistance from the Corporation. In urban areas, the income limit was Rs. 4,300 per annum for eligibility to get loan and assistance from the Corporation.

Activities of GSCEDC

(a) The Corporation expects the nationalised banks to provide financial assistance to scheduled caste families for different income generating schemes. The bank advances loans to the target groups under differential rates of interest for the purpose of bringing them above the poverty line. Under this scheme, the Corporation deposits 25.00 per cent of the money so advanced with respective banks as a margin money. The Corporation disburses the portion of the margin money only after the bank sanctions the loans to the beneficiary. Moreover, the Corporation provides direct finances to individual persons of scheduled castes households, specially where the nationalised banks have not taken up this responsibility. In special cases where the households of scheduled castes were most down-trodden and where the banks found it difficult to advance money, the corporation directly advances loans to them. The maximum amount to be advanced to households on non-recurring basis was Rs. 12,000 and the loan repayable in 4 years with the interest rate of 4.00 per cent and subsidy at the rate of Rs. 750 per beneficiary.

(b) There is a wide range of programmes for financial assistance to the industrial cooperative societies formed by the scheduled castes. The terms and conditions for the establishment of such a society have already been laid down by the Corporation which provides the working capital loan at the rate of 4.00 per cent interest for one year to such cooperative societies. In the same way, the Corporation provides financial assistance to Labour Contract Co-operative

Societies for scheduled castes. It may be noted that there is a provision of providing subsidy to the Bamboo Cooperative Societies only.

(c) The Corporation has also a special scheme for auto-rickshaw owners in order that they become self-employed licensed driver. The people, who are eligible for this scheme, are given easy credit to be repaid over a period of time. However, a person has to be in possession of a driving licence for auto-rickshaw and has to have arranged to buy the vehicle from a recognised dealer. The annual income of such persons from all sources has not to exceed Rs. 4,300.00 in urban areas and Rs. 3,500.00 in rural areas.

Targets of GSCEDC for 1983-84

The Corporation was given the target of giving assistance to 50,000 families belonging to the scheduled castes during 1983-84. For this purpose, a plan was drawn at district, taluka and village levels. It had to take care of the households of scheduled castes below the poverty line both in Special Component Plan area and Non-Special Component Plan area.

From the gereral review of literature throwing light on the activities of the Corporation it seems that a lot had to be done in order to spread its activities in rural areas.

It is suggested that the Corporation should open special branches at district and taluka levels to reach the needy households at village level as quickly as possible. Moreover, it will go a long way in furthering the cause of households below the poverty line if the Corporation creates a band of voluntary workers who can educate the people of scheduled castes regarding the benefits offered to them for economic development. The Corporation should, therefore, hold training programmes for young scheduled castes boys and girls who can take up the programme of educating families by visiting them in the villages over a period of time.

12

OBSERVATIONS AND RECOMMENDATIONS

The observations and recommendations of this study are rounded up to the extent possible in order to suit the requirements and the objects of the study. The social climate in Gujarat State is by and large healthy with regard to the relations between the members of scheduled castes and the people of other communities. However, there have been occasions when disturbance cropped up. They have done a lot of damage to the fair name of Gujarat.

(1) It appears that when vigorous public announcements are made while providing special benefits to scheduled castes, situations have arisen when tensions developed in the minds of the poor and disadvantaged people of other communities. At the time of implementation of Land Ceiling Act, Tenancy Legislation, Debt Redemption Act, 20-Point Programme, reservation of seats in institutions, etc., the social climate was surcharged with antagonism towards the secheduled castes. Such situations resulted into unfortunate violence and deaths. After the lapse of some time each one of these schemes and reform movements was found to have been bogged down in administrative procedures and delays on account of divergent interpretations of actions required for implementation at ground level. There have been also pre-meditated plans by some sections or individuals of the high castes to vitiate the aims and objectives of implementing the sehemes.

It may be noted that in the case of reservations of seats for scheduled castes for admission into educational institutions and jobs, tempers went up at a point of time in certain urban areas of Gujarat. The results of these agitations in 1981 were to be found in clashes between the people of two communities. The impact of such clashes in the urban areas created back-lash in the rural areas of contiguous regions. It was unfortunate that in some cases, the poorer members of scheduled castes, who were really disadvantaged from the gains of reservations, had to suffer in rural areas for no fault of their own.

(2) The spread of education among the scheduled castes is not commensurate with the increase in population of these communities. This is the reason why the younger people of scheduled castes looking for jobs remained incapable of entering into skilled or semi-skilled jobs other than those of agricultural labour.

It was , therefore, recommended that incentives be provided to poor scheduled castes households for sending their children to school by way of providing free food grains for each child sent to school. This incentive should be equivalent to the earnings of a child, boy or girl, who is regularly sent by the households for earning daily wages.

(3) The study has revealed that there were a handful of viable landholders among scheduled castes and very few of them were able to earn their full livelihood from cultivation of land. The land reforms introduced by the State to help the depressed classes acquire enough land of their own, for self cultivation have not really benefitted a large number of them. Whoever has been able to get land from the government schemes, Bhoodan and other movements, the plots of land were not sizeable and, therefore, not of real asset to them. If a household gets 2 to 3 acres of land from the government or other sources, it is not likely to be of good quality and , therefore, some of them openly said that such gifts became liabilities rather than assets to them.

(4) It seems that the position of providing surplus land to landless scheduled castes members and members of other depressed classes through Tenancy Legislation has nearly become redundant. For, most of such cases of tenants claiming right over the land under their cultivation and possession have possibly been settled in the court of law, or through concealed negotiations. On the other hand, the Ceiling Act is found to be defective in many respects. The manner in which the implementation of this act is being thwarted by the landholders, defy imagination. The acquision of surplus land by government through implementing Ceiling Act has not become fully successful.

If in future, the government desires to create conditions for acquiring large areas of surplus land through Ceiling Act, it is recommended to lower down the ceiling size permissible to a landholder. Such a step could be justified in the areas and regions where the government has developmental plans to make heavy investment, through agricultural incentives, providing irrigation and a number of inputs and facilities including credits, seeds, fertilizers and implements.

There are bound to be differences from place to place with regard to ecological and soil conditions . It is necessary, therefore, to frame a flexible policy with regard to lowering minimum ceiling from 30 acres to be held by a household. The implementation of Ceiling Act calls for consensus on the part of political elites and landholding gentry, specially in the manner in which differential pattern of ceiling is fixed by the government from time to time and from area to area.

(5) It was reported that the system of administering Land Ceiling Act was very sluggish and time consuming. It has certain defects which create difficulty in giving advantage to those in need of land. It was, therefore, recommended to critically examine it with a view to remove handicaps in the way of smooth implementation of the programme. There was no systematic monitoring of execution of the act. It was further recommended that the government appoint a Task Force which can move from place to place and look into the distribution of surplus land in appropriate manner.

(6) The study revealed that the mortgage of land of scheduled castes and other weaker sections of the society was replete with irregularities and underhand dealings by the moneylenders. Such practices were indulged in by the people concerned with connivance or in collusion with intermediaries in and outside government administration.

One of the glaring and outright illegal practice was noticed in the manner in which land mortgage deeds were worked out. A number of such deeds were signed on a piece of plain paper without court fee stamp of lesser value than one prescribed for the purpose. The value of stamps is determined in accordance with the amount of transation, size and quality of land mortgaged by the landholders. The fair and normal practices are violated by the moneylenders with impunity.

It was, therefore, recommended that the government take immediate steps to issue a notification in order to make immediate seizure of all such illegal documents and effect restoration of land to the bonafide poor occupants coming from depressed classes. In all cases where the names of the original occupants were to be found intact in 7—12 columns of the Village Form of Revenue Department, the Government should make necessary investigations if land was mortgaged illegally by the moneylender.

(7) The study revealed that a large number of scheduled castes households were earning their livelihood by practising agricultural labour in the fields of others. They lived more or less hand to mouth. They were not able to get suitable house sites for building houses to protect the members of their households. The scheme of allotment of house sites to these people had many loopholes, as a result of which a number of scheduled castes households did not become eligible for receiving free house sites. The figures provided by the government from time to time, indicating the number of plots distributed for house sites, did not give the total picture .

The success of house sites programme should be assessed on the actual number of households who built houses on the plots along with the facility of road, street light, etc., suitable to minimum standard of living. It was, therefore, recommended that the Land Committee at the taluka level, which looks into house sites programmes, be strengthened by including at least two members of the scheduled castes to protect their interests.

(8) Integrated Rural Development Programme is one of the major strategies for development of poor sections of the society in rural areas. However, IRD benefits had not reached members of scheduled castes as desired. It was, threfore, recommended that the state government appoint a Task Force to review the whole programme and find out how much benefits have gone to households of the poor and also suggest remedial measures to improve the programme.

(9) In some villages, where irrigation was introduced gradually over a long period of time, the low lying areas had sometimes developed into Kharland. Such waste land area which may belong to the poor class of the people in rural areas become a liability to them. It was, therefore, recommended that the State Government identify such households suffering from disability of this nature, and help reclaim their land by scientific method of restoration so that the fertility of the soil was restored.

(10) It was observed that the beneficiaries of house sites some times got their plots either far away from the village or not suitable for residential purpose due to water logging, uneven surface of the land, etc. It was, therefore, recommended that as far as possible

house sites to the landless laboureres of the scheduled castes be given in the close vicinity of the village, and if possible near the residential locality of high caste people.

(11) The scourge of untouchability was reported to be practised in some villages. This, however, had to be removed especially from the village schools where younger generation of the scheduled castes were taking education. If the teachers and students were not able to forget the barriers of castism on account of untouchability, the evil would continue to perpetuate for a long period of time. It was, therefore, recommended that the government order District Panchayats to provide facility of a common place of drinking water in all the primary schools without differentiating between communities with respect to use of drinking water, tumblers and pots.

(12) It was revealed from the study that the use of new technology, inputs, etc., could not be easily adopted by the landholders of scheduled castes because most of them had small plots of land. The other reasons why they were not able to invest more in the land, were poor quality of land, difficulty in getting irrigation facilities, loans and subsidies in time. It was, therefore, recommended that the government machinery try to see that no landholder from the scheduled castes remained disadvantaged from getting help for agriculture on account of administrative or other reasons.

(13) The income of scheduled castes derived from agricultural labour was not adequate because the wages fixed for agricultural labour by the government were not generally paid. Moreover, this being a seasonal occupation for poor households of scheduled castes, they had to suffer on account of under-employment or unemployment out of agricultural season. It was, therefore, suggested that the occupational pattern for scheduled castes be rapidly changed in rural areas by way of creating job opportunities in small scale industries and cottage industries.

(14) Some scheduled castes people were getting their livelihood from animal husbandry, service, etc. It was revealed from the study that those households who were engaged in service and animal husbandry were able to earn livelihood slightly better than those engaged in labourous occupations. It was, therefore, recommended that the Special Component Plan prepare a programme by which the disadvantage households of scheduled castes undertake seasonal migration to contiguous semi-urban or urban areas, where processing and cottage industries centres are developed under government

patronage.

(15) With respect to the pattern of indebtedness, it was found that a large number of scheduled castes households did not depend heavily as before on private moneylenders for borrowing money. It is significant to note that among private money lenders there is no exclusive community such as Bania and others involved in the transactions. The families of other communities who became well-to-do after Independence had also taken up to private moneylending. It was recommended in this context that registration of money lenders be insisted upon strictly in rural areas so that the poor people are not exploited by a new class of usurious moneylenders.

(16) With regard to methods of identification of poverty line for the people in rural areas, some scholars thought that the calorie intake of individuals be able to tell whether the family was living below the poverty line. This method suffers from the fallacy of time factor because at different points of time in a year, there may not be uniformity in calorie-in-take of all the members in a family becasue ritual fasts, etc., associated with the traditional social behaviour.

(17) The method of per capita income as the main yardstick to measure poverty also suffers from time factor fallacy, because generally the members of the poor households in rural areas have irregular employment opportunities and, therefore, irratic income. There are also other approaches to identify poverty of a household on the basis of levels of living and employment structure of members of the family. It was recommended that factors of calorie-in-take, per capita income, levels of living, etc., could be amalgamated in such a way that it becomes realistic to determine poverty line in rural areas.

(18) The awareness and knowledge of the Special Component Plan providing easy loan facilities from the Scheduled Castes Economic Development Corporation, Scheduled Banks, etc., had not reached the needy households. It was, therefore, recommended that the SC Economic Development Corporation open up subsidiary branches at the District and Taluka levels so that its benefits go to scheduled castes households in villages. It was further recommended that the Corporation give not only economic assistance and training to a band of voluntary workers of younger generation of scheduled castes for propagating its goals, but also for those who can use their training and knowledge for providing literacy and general education to scheduled castes families from village to village.

APPENDIX I

District-Wise Population of Scheduled-Castes In Gujarat 1981

Sr. No.	District	Total Population of the Dist.	Population of S.Cs. in the District	Propotion of S.Cs. population in the Dist.	Proportion of the S.Cs. population in the State
1.	2.	3.	4.	5.	6.
1.	Ahmedabad	38,75,794	4,36,937	11.27	17.91
2.	Amreli	10,79,097	93,048	8.62	3.82
3.	Banaskantha	16,67,914	1,70,141	10.20	6.98
4.	Baroda	25,58,092	1,53,689	6.01	6.30
5.	Broach	12,96,451	59,693	4.60	2.45
6.	Bhavnagar	18,79,340	99,757	5.31	4.09
7.	Dangs	1,13,664	750	0.66	0.03
8.	Jamnagar	13,93,076	1,01,619	7.29	4.17
9.	Junagadh	21,00,709	1,76,595	8.40	7.24
10.	Kaira	30,15,027	1,77,072	5.87	7.26
11.	Kutch	10,50,161	1,11,882	10.65	4.59
12.	Mehsana	25,48,787	2,23,044	8.75	9.15
13.	Gandhinagar	2,89,088	21,119	7.33	0.87
14.	Panchmahal	23,21,689	88,232	3.80	3.62
15.	Rajkot	20,93,094	1,37,033	6.55	5.62
16.	Sabarkantha	15,02,284	1,28,540	8.56	5.27
17.	Surat	24,93,211	91,642	3.68	3.76
18.	Surendranagar	10,34,185	1,12,435	10.87	4.61
19.	Valsad	17,74,136	54,989	3.10	2.26
	Grand Total	3,40,85,799	24,38,297	7.15	—

APPENDIX II

Population of Scheduled Castes in Sample Taluka-1981

Sr. No.	Taluka	Total population of the taluka	Population of S.Cs. in the taluka	Proportion of S.Cs. population in the taluka	Proportion of the S.Cs. population in the Dist.
1.	2.	3.	4.	5.	6.
(1)	**Ahmedabad District**				
1.	Ahmedabad	25,30,920	2,93,845	11.61	67.25
2.	Daskroi	2,78,107	21,931	7.89	5.02
3.	Dholka	2,61,092	39,682	15.20	9.08
4.	Dhandhuka	2,13,748	21,881	10.25	5.01
5.	Sanand	1,37,346	17,491	12.73	4.01
6.	Viramgam	2,70,948	31,505	11.63	7.21
7.	Dehgam	1,83,633	10,602	5.77	2.42
	Total	38,75,794	4,36,937	11.27	(100.00)
(2)	**Amreli District**				
1.	Amreli	1,76,233	13,106	7.44	14.09
2.	Dhari	1,26,581	10,489	8.31	11.27
3.	Khambha-Mahal	76,556	2,423	5.20	2.60
4.	Rajula	1,32,268	9,667	7.31	10.39
5.	Jafrabad-Mahal	59,153	3,799	6.42	4.08
6.	Kodinar	1,38,970	23,471	16.89	25.23
7.	Kunkavav	1,53,092	13,859	9.05	14.89
8.	Babara	91,911	6,149	6.69	6.61
9.	Lathi	1,00,487	6,861	6.83	7.38
10.	Lalia-Mahala	53,846	3,224	5.66	3.46
	Total	10,79,097	93,045	8.62	(100.00)

* Sample Talukas.

1.	2.	3.	4.	5.	6.
(3)	**Banaskantha District**				
1.	Palanpur	3,07,683	29,703	9.65	17.46
2.	Vadgam	1,38,752	23,240	16.75	13.66
3.	Deesa	2,60,532	23,859	9.17	14.04
4.	Kankarej	1,47,201	10,459	7.11	6.15
5.	Radhanpur	81,174	6,940	8.55	4.08
6.	Santalpur	72,619	5,087	7.01	2.99
7.	Deodar	1,45,075	12,474	8.60	7.33
8.	Vav	1,22,915	18,117	14.74	10.65
9.	Tharad	1,47,830	19,183	12.98	11.27
10.	Dhanara	1,42,288	1,676	11.74	9.82
11.	Danta	1,01,845	4,337	4.26	2.55
	Total	16,67,914	1,70,141	10.20	(100.00)
(4)	**Baroda District**				
1.	Baroda	9,91,597	67,290	6.78	43.78
2.	Karjan	1,37,314	11,042	8.04	7.18
3.	Padra	2,01,610	15,677	7.78	10.20
4.	Savli	1,93,613	11,700	6.04	7.61
5.	Vaghodia	1,05,009	5,396	5.14	3.51
6.	Dabhoi	1,64,397	12,955	7.88	8.43
7.	Sankheda	1,49,311	7,557	5.06	4.92
8.	Jetpur-Pavi	1,67,473	4,080	2.44	2.65
9.	Chhota-Udepur	2,40,699	7,716	3.21	5.02
10.	Naswadi	89,263	1,719	1.93	1.12
11.	Tilakwada	48,661	2,665	5.46	1.73
12.	Sinor	69,145	5,902	8.54	3.84
	Total	25,58,092	1,53,689	6.01	(100.00)
(5)	**Bharuch District**				
1.	Bharuch	2,65,093	16,053	6.06	26.89
2.	Ankleshwar	1,28,644	4,807	3.74	8.05
3.	Hansot	50,245	3,835	7.63	6.42
4.	Vagra	65,487	4,245	6.48	7.11
5.	Jambusar	1,58,346	13,294	8.39	22.27
6.	Amod	79,934	5,155	6.45	8.67

1.	2.	3.	4.	5.	6.
7.	Jhagadia	1,28,134	3,928	3.07	6.58
8.	Nandod	1,79,263	6,460	3.60	10.82
9.	Dediapada	88,431	619	0.70	1.04
10.	Sagbara	58,584	489	0.83	0.82
11.	Valia	94,319	808	0.86	1.36
	Total	12,96,451	59,693	40.60	(100.00
(6)	**Dangs District**				
1.	Dang	1,13,664	750	0.66	0.66
(This is a special tribal district without any taluka subdivisions.)					
(7)	**Bhavnagar District**				
1.	Bhavnagar	4,07,032	18,542	4.56	18.59
2.	Ghogha-Mahal	63,481	2,379	3.75	2.38
3.	Talaja	1,82,541	7,661	4.20	7.69
4.	Mahuva	2,64,155	10,760	4.07	10.79
5.	Kundala	2,08,426	12,942	6.21	12.97
6.	Gariyadhar	89,078	5,000	5.61	5.01
7.	Palitana	1,39,591	7,923	5.68	7.95
8.	Sinor	1,32,483	8,932	6.74	8.96
9.	Umrala	72,401	5.686	7.85	5.70
10.	Gadhada	1,23,823	6,968	5.63	6.98
11.	Botad	1,32,874	9,282	6.99	9.30
12.	Vallabhipur	63,455	3,676	5.79	3.68
	Total	1,879,340	99,757	5.31	(100.00)
(8)	**Jamnagar District**				
1.	Jamnagar	4,72,482	30,284	6.41	29.80
2.	Lalpur	88,123	6,980	7.92	6.87
3.	Jam-Jodhpur	1,10,266	10,060	9.12	9.90
4.	Bhanvad	92,403	6,758	7.31	6.65
5.	Kalyanpur	1,20,194	6,701	5.58	6.59
6.	Okhamandal	93,543	10,632	11.37	10.46
7.	Khambhaliya	1,47,632	7,766	5.26	7.64
8.	Jodiya	83,422	4,993	5.99	4.91
9.	Dhrol	58,137	5,820	10.01	5.73

1.	2.	3.	4.	5.	6.
10.	Kalavad	1,26,874	11,631	9.17	11.45
	Total	13,93,076	1,01,619	7.29	(100.00)
(9)	**Junagadh District**				
1.	Junagadh	2,43,280	17,567	7.22	9.95
2.	Mendarde	58,294	4,758	8.16	2.69
3.	Talala	91,667	6,179	6.74	3.50
4.	Patan-Veraval	2,60,578	23,474	9.01	13.29
5.	Malia	1,10,966	8,590	7.74	4.86
6.	Mangrol	1,43,474	14,602	10.18	8.27
7.	Keshod	1,36,677	13,746	10.06	7.78
8.	Porbandar	2,70,972	19,866	7.33	11.26
9.	Ranavav	75,205	7,617	10.13	4.31
10.	Kutiyana	79,712	8,416	10.56	4.77
11.	Manavadar	1,25,302	13,195	10.53	7.47
12.	Vanthali	95,980	10,567	11.01	5.98
13.	Bhesen-Mahal	66,596	4,895	7.35	2.77
14.	Visavadar	1,18,309	6,655	5.63	3.77
15.	Una	2,23,687	16,468	7.36	9.33
	Total	21,00,709	1,76,595	8.40	(100.00)
(10)	**Kaira District**				
1.	Mehmdabad	2,12,869	13,000	6.10	7.35
2.	Anand	5,12,449	19,595	3.82	11.06
3.	Nadiad	4,71,916	20,503	4.34	11.58
4.	Petlad	3,06,472	21,630	7.06	12.21
5.	Borsad	3,71,211	19,403	5.23	10.90
6.	Khambhat	2,63,373	23,934	9.09	13.52
7.	Metar	1,60,810	13,555	8.43	7.66
8.	Kapadwanj	3,19,691	18,377	5.75	10.38
9.	Balasinor	1,61,535	12,877	7.97	7.28
10.	Thasara	2,34,701	14,278	6.08	8.06
	Total	30,15,027	1,17,072	5.87	(100.00)

1.	2.	3.	4.	5.	6.
(11)	**Kutch District**				
1.	Bhuj	2,16,318	18,428	8.52	16.47
2.	Mundra	63,224	10,076	15.94	9.01
3.	Mandvi	1,30,146	14,401	11.07	12.87
4.	Abdasa	78,982	7,549	9.56	6.75
5.	Lakhpat	28,902	2,781	9.62	2.48
6.	Nakhtrana	1,05,900	12,336	11.65	11.03
7.	Rapar	1,35,049	12,531	9.89	7.96
8.	Bhachau	1,00,252*	8,908	8.89	7.96
9.	Anjar	1,19,388	24,872	13.00	22.23
	Total	10,50,161	1,11,882	10.65	(100.00)

* Sample talukas

1.	2.	3.	4.	5.	6.
(12)	**Mehsana District**				
1.	Mehsana	3,06,374	25,228	8.23	11.31
2.	Kadi	2,16,266	20,268	9.37	9.09
3.	Chanasma	2,07,607	18,455	8.91	8.29
4.	Sami	1,28,315	13,667	10.65	6.13
5.	Harij	69,101	6,638	9.59	2.98
6.	Patan	3,03,944	30,124	9.91	13.51
7.	Sidhpur	2,88,106	25,574	8.88	11.47
8.	Kheralu	2,46,485	20,684	8.39	9.27
9.	Visnagar	1,98,873	15,289	7.69	6.85
10.	Vijapur	3,63,649	26,257	7.22	11.77
11.	Kalol	2,20,067	20,829	9.46	9.33
	Total	25,48,787	2,23,044	8.75	(100.00)
(13)	**Gandhinagar District**				
1.	Gandhinagar	2,89,088	21,199	7.33	7.33

(This is a special district with State Capital, like the Dangs)

1.	2.	3.	4.	5.	6.
(14)	**Panchmahals District**				
1.	Godhra	3,41,991	17,753	5.19	20.12
2.	Kalol	1,43,913	10,579	7.35	11.99
3.	Halol	1,31,430	3,843	2.92	4.36
4.	Shehera	1,42,421	7,681	5.39	8.71

1.	2.	3.	4.	5.	6.
5.	Lunawada	2,30,777	16,351	7.09	18.53
6.	Santrampur	3,23,268	9,092	2.81	10.30
7.	Jhalod	2,00,445	3,229	1.61	3.66
8.	Dohad	2,96,322	7,738	2.61	8.77
9.	Limkheda	2,11,470	3,328	1.57	3.77
10.	Devgadh-Baria	2,75,104	8,225	2.99	9.32
11.	Jambughodha	24,548	413	1.68	0.47
	Total	23,21,689	88,232	3.80	(100.00)

* Sample talukas

(15) **Rajkot District**

1.	Rajkot	5,66,581	29,821	5.26	21.76
2.	Kotda-Sangani	51,671	7,860	9.41	3.55
3.	Gondal	2,12,665	14,544	6.84	10.61
4.	Jetpur	1,74,040	10,712	6.15	7.82
5.	Dhoraji	1,51,681	11,018	7.26	8.04
6.	Upleta	1,70,609	14,811	8.68	10.81
7.	Jam-Kandarna	63,661	5,909	9.28	4.31
8.	Lodhika-Mahal	37,711	4,242	11.25	3.10
9.	Padhhari	65,458	5,990	9.15	4.37
10.	Morvi	2,45,165	16,761	6.84	12.23
11.	Malia	62,777	3,100	4.94	2.26
12.	Wankaner	1,22,454	6,816	5.57	4.97
13.	Jasdan	1,68,621	8,449	5.01	6.17
	Total	20,93,014	1,37,033	6.55	(100.00)

(16) **Sabarkantha District**

1.	Himatnagar	1,88,426	20,916	11.10	16.27
2.	Prantij	2,16,926	18,316	8.44	14.25
3.	Idar	2,41,960	35,580	14.70	27.68
4.	Khedbrahma	1,36,044	6,094	4.48	4.74
5.	Vijaynagar	58,776	3,561	6.06	2.77
6.	Bhiloda	1,46,114	8,853	6.05	6.89
7.	Meghraj	91,437	3,423	3.74	2.66
8.	Modasa	1,92,007	15,975	8.32	12.43
9.	Malpur	64,204	4,387	6.83	3.41

1.	2.	3.	4.	5.	6.
10.	Bayad	1,66,372	11,435	6.87	8.90
	Total	15,02,284	1,28,540	8.56	(100.00)
(17)	**Surat District**				
1.	Chorasi	10,87,482	52,835	4.86	57.65
2.	Olpad	1,34,048	6,628	4.94	7.23
3.	Kamrej	1,08,307	6,746	6.23	7.36
4.	Mangrol	1,62,113	6,188	3.82	6.75
5.	Mandvi	1,37,727	1,787	1.30	1.95
6.	Songadh	1,46,227	1,205	0.82	1.31
7.	Uchhchal	52,692	65	0.12	0.07
8.	Nizar	80,683	1,913	2.37	2.09
9.	Vyara	1,82,078	1,710	0.94	1.87
10.	Valod	66,291	812	1.22	0.89
11.	Bardoli	1,55,274	5,793	3.73	6.32
12.	Mahuva	1,04,241	2,318	2.22	2.53
	Total	24,93,211	91,642	3.68	(100.00)
(18)	**Surendranagar District**				
*1.	Surendranagar	2,06,552	20,611	9.98	18.33
2.	Limbadi	1,78,267	23,595	13.24	20.99
3.	Sayala	61,223	4,689	7.66	4.17
4.	Chotila	98,526	9,031	9.17	8.03
*5.	Muli	68,466	7,494	10.95	6.67
*6.	Halvad	90,257	5,895	6.53	5.24
7.	Dhrangadhra	1,37,171	14,008	10.21	12.46
*8.	Dasada	1,37,389	19,193	13.97	17.07
9.	Lakhatar	56,334	7,919	14.06	7.04
	Total	10,34,185	1,12,435	10.87	(100.00)

* Sample talukas

1.	2.	3.	4.	5.	6.
(19)	**Valsad District**				
1.	Valsad	2,78,033	9,340	3.36	16.99
2.	Pardi	2,05,538	7,344	3.57	13.36
3.	Umbergaon	1,43,727	7,499	5.22	13.64
4.	Gandevi	1,90,049	7,474	3.93	13.59
5.	Naswadi	3,59,797	15,118	4.20	27.48
6.	Chikhli	2,14,128	5,902	2.75	10.73
7.	Bansda	1,45,791	966	0.66	1.76
8.	Dharmpur	2,37,073	1,346	0.57	2.45
	Total	17,74,136	54,989	3.10	(100.00)

APPENDIX - III

Selection of Sample Villages on the basis of high, medium and low percentages of S.C. Population.

Sr. No.	Taluka		Village	Percentage of S.C. population Type	Percentage	No.of families selected for study
1.	2.		3.	4.	5.	6.
1.	**Ahmedabad District**					
1.	Viramgam	1	Shahpur	L	4.4	5
		2	Rudatal	M	10.8	5
		3	Sadatpura	H	12.0	5
2.	Dholka	1	Koharia	L	4.8	5
		2	Begva	M	6.6	5
		3	Ingoli	H	16.2	5
3.	Dehgam	1	Kadjodara	L	4.4	5
		2	Halisa	M	6.2	5
		3	Vasana Rathod	H	13.0	5
4.	Dhandhuka	1	Motivadadi	L	4.2	5
		2	Jalila	M	8.5	5
		3	Khokharnesh	H	13.3	5

Note : L = Low M = Medium H = High

Sr. No.	Taluka		Village	Type	Percentage	No.of families selected for study
2.	**Kaira District**					
1.	Khambhat	1	Nagra	L	4.9	5
		2	Tarapur	M	6.2	5
		3	Kashbara	H	32.1	5
2.	Petlad	1	Petali	L	4.0	5
		2	Demol	M	8.1	5

1.	2.		3.	4.	5.	6.
		3	Dawalpura	H	12.1	5
3.	Anand	1	Boriawi	H	3.0	6
		2	Khanpur	M	8.9	5
		3	Gana	L	12.9	5
4.	Kapadwanj	1	Mundel	L	4.4	5
		2	Chhipdi	M	8.6	5
		3	Lalpar	H	25.2	5
3.	**Mehsana District**					
1.	Sami	1	Gajdinpura	L	4.5	5
		2	Dadka	M	8.9	5
		3	Gujarwada	H	11.5	5
2.	Sidhpur	1	Vaghrol	L	4.4	5
		2	Amudh	M	8.6	5
		3	Chatawada	H	25.2	5
3.	Vijapur	1	Bapupura	L	6.0	5
		2	Manekpur	M	8.2	5
		3	Rangpur	H	11.6	5
4.	Harij	1	Ro-da	L	4.6	5
		2	Kureja	M	8.2	5
		3	Juna Kalana	H	25.4	5
4.	**Surendranagar District**					
1.	Wadhwan	1	Bala	L	5.6	5
		2	Kharwa	M	9.7	5
		3	Rajper	H	4.2	5
2.	Halvad	1	Ratabhe	L	4.0	5
		2	Juna Devalia	M	6.5	5
		3	Isanpur	H	17.0	5
3.	Dasada	1	Bhalgam	L	3.1	5
		2	Gawana	M	10.4	5
		3	Visavadi	H	32.1	5
4.	Muli	1	Tidana	L	5.2	5
		2	Leeya	M	7.4	5
		3	Ambardi	H	17.3	5

BIBLIOGRAPHY

Aiyappan, A., *Social Revolution in Kerala Village*, Asia, Bombay, 1966.

Ambedkar, B.R., *The Untouchables*, Amrit Book Co., New Delhi, 1948.

Ambedkar, B.R., *Who were the Shudras*, Thacker & Co., Bombay, 1971.

Beteille, Andre, *Inequality and Social Change*, Oxford, Delhi, 1972.

Census of India, 1961, Volume I, part V-B, Part XI-D, B.K.Roy Burman, Delhi, 1970, etc.

Chitnis, Suma, *Literacy and Educational Enrolement among the Scheduled Castes of Maharashtra*, Tata Institute of Social Sciences, Bombay, 1974.

Cohn, Bernard S., "Madhopur Revisited," *Economic and Political Weekly*, July, 1959.

Desai, I.P., *Water Facilities for the Untouchables in Rural Gujarat*, ICSSR, New Delhi 1973.

Fuchs, Stephen, *The Children of Hari*, Alllahabad, 1949.

Gandhi, M.K., *All Men are Brothers*, etc., Ed., Krishna Kriplani, Ahmedabad, 1966.

India, Committee on Welfare of SCs and STs, First Report, Lok Sabha Secretariate, New Delhi, 1969, Second part to Twentieth Report 1969 to 1973.

Kamble, N.D., *Scheduled Castes*, New Delhi, 1982.

Kananaikil, Jose, *Scheduled Castes and the struggle against Inequality*, New Delhi, 1983.

Khan, Mumtaz Ali, *Scheduled Castes and their Status in India*, New Delhi, 1980.

Lynch, Owen M., *The Politics of Untouchability*, Columbia, 1969.

Mahar, J. Michael, Ed., *Untouchables in Contemporary India*, Arizona, 1971.

Makwana, Yogendra and Shantaben, "How Dark is the Shadow", and "From Lending Money to Grabbing Land", *Parishad Sandesh*, Vol. I, No. 5, New Delhi, 1983.

Malkani, M.R., *Clean People and Unclean Country*, Harijan Sevak Sangh, Delhi, 1965.

Murthy, B.S., *Depressed, and Oppressed; Their Economic and Social Conditions,* S. Chand, Delhi, 1972.

Naik, J.P., *Education of Scheduled Castes*, ICSSR, New Delhi, 1972.

Nayak, Dahyabhai, *Gujaratman Harijan Kalyan Pravrutti*, (in Gujarati), Gandhinagar, 1975.

Patel, Urmilaben C., *Vikasta Samudayo* (in Gujarati), Mangal Prabhat Publishers, Ahmedabad, 1983.

Parvathamma, C., *Scheduled Castes and Tribes : A Socio-Economic Survey*, New Delhi, 1984.

Patwardhan, Sunanda, *Change among India's Harijans*, Orient Longman, Bombay, 1973.

Sachchidananda, *Status of the Scheduled Castes with Special Reference to Change*, ICSSR, New Delhi, 1971.

Shrikant, L.M., "Scheduled Castes and their Welfare", in M.S.Gore Ed., *Enclopaedia of Social Work in India*, Vol.2, Delhi, 1968.

Thapar, Romesh, *Seminar 177*, The Untouchables, New Delhi, May 1974.

Tiwari, Chitra, *Shudras in Manu*, Motilal Banarsidas, Delhi, 1963.

Trivedi, H.R. and Bhakta, S.K., "Implications of Social Legislation Pertaining to Scheduled Castes in Gujarat", in *Social Administration, Development and Change*, Eds. T.N. Chaturvedi and MS. S.K. Chandra, I.I. P.A, New Delhi, 1980.

Trivedi, H.R., *Scheduled Castes Women : Studies in Exploitation*, Concept Publishing Company, New Delhi, 1977.

INDEX